DOLLS

ANTONIA FRASER

 OCTOPUS BOOKS

Acknowledgments

The author wishes to acknowledge with grateful thanks the special help she has received from the following people: Miss Irene Blair Hickman, Leslie Daiken Esq, Mrs Graham Greene, and Councillor Patrick Murray of the Museum of Childhood, Edinburgh.

The author and publishers wish to thank the following owners who have made available dolls from their collections: Mrs Lovat Fraser, figure 17; Major Leo Plummer, 22; Admiral Sir Herbert Meade-Fetherstonhaugh, 18; Mrs Graham Greene, 40, 67, 87, 91, 126, 127; Miss Irene Blair Hickman, 43, 61, 65, 71, 110; Mrs Fox-Hunter and Mrs E. Transdell, 58; Mrs E. Ingham, 69; John Noble Esq, 85, 89; Mr and Mrs Joshua Logan, 103, 104, 108; Mrs Margaret Hutchings, 115; Mr Roger Field, 118; Colonel A.J.K. Todd, 130; Miss Katherine McClure-Smith, 136; Miss E. Mould, 100.

The following photographs are reproduced by courtesy of the following museums and institutions: Museum of Childhood, Edinburgh, figures 1, 5, 6, 54, 77, 81, 82, 84; British Museum, 2, 3, 4, 8, 9, 10, 11, 12, 15, 16; Pollock's Toy Museum, London, 7, 13, 14, 28, 36, 47, 85, 113, 116, 135, 138, 139; Musée des Arts Decoratifs, Paris, 30, 44, 45, 46, 57, 96; Victoria & Albert Museum, London, 19, 24, 52, 83, 134; Joy Robinson Collection, Warwick Doll Museum, 32, 38, 70, 88, 94, 106; Bethnal Green Museum, London, 23, 60, 62, 64, 78, 100, 138; Rijksmuseum, Amsterdam, 33, 34, 42, 51, 86; London Museum 27, 29, 50, 68, 72, 88, 107, 109, 119, 129; Radio Times Hulton Picture Library, 26, 48, 62; Salisbury, South Wiltshire and Blackmore Museum, 39; New York Historical Society, New York City, 31, 41, 53, 63, 99; Smithsonian Institution, Washington D. C., 35, 79, 112; Museum of the City of New York, 37, 49, 56; Toy Museum, Rottingdean, 59, 75, 95, 111, 114, 128; Cercle Français de Protection de l'Enfance, Paris, 66, 74, 124; The Rocking Horse, London, 76; Musée de l'Histoire de l'Éducation, Paris, 92, 102 (Collection Sieu); Bethnal Green Public Library, London, 78; Brooklyn Children's Museum, New York, 120, 121, 122, 123, 140; Danish Folk Museum, Copenhagen, 125, 131, 132, 133; and the National Trust, 18.

Figure 130 was photographed by Desmond Tripp; 1, 5, 6, 54, 77, 81, 82, 84 by Norward Inglis; 7, 13, 14, 18, 19, 23, 24, 28, 36, 43, 47, 50, 52, 60, 61, 64, 65, 71, 78, 83, 85, 89, 100, 105, 110, 113, 116, 134, 135, 136, 137, 138, 139 by Messrs A. C. Cooper; 17, 59, 75, 76, 95, 111, 114, 117, 128 by Anthony Panting; 22, 55, 60, 73 by Angus McBean; 32, 38, 70, 88, 94, 106 by Walter Scott; 39 by John Champion; 40, 67, 87, 91, 126, 127 by Jonathan Green-Armytage; 66, 74, 124 by Studio Nestlé, Paris. 80, 93, 98 were supplied by Leslie Daiken Esq.

This edition first published 1973 by
OCTOPUS BOOKS LIMITED
59 Grosvenor Street, London W 1

ISBN O 7064 0056 9

Produced by Mandarin Publishers Limited
77a Marble Road, North Point, Hong Kong
and printed in Hong Kong

Preceding page
Two walking dolls of the late nineteenth century made by the famous Jumeau family at Montreuil in France.

Contents

1 A Balinese votive doll made of dried palm-leaves about 1880. Figures like this were given to children to play with once their religious significance had faded.

Early History

THE OLDEST DOLL-LIKE FIGURES to survive the slaughter of the centuries were not dolls at all but religious images, mainly of a funereal nature, and consequently very far removed from the child's plaything as later generations were to know it. The existence of such objects of magico-religious significance has led some scholars to assert that the doll form existed for thousands of years before the child first took possession of it. They point to the fact that no dolls have been discovered in children's graves of the prehistoric period, and consider it unlikely that at a time when men believed in the magical properties of the artificial human figure, mere children should have been permitted to play with objects so wrapped in mysteries.

The most famous examples of these early talismans are the *Ushabti* or funeral figures of the ancient Egyptian civilization. Once hailed by experts as prototypes of early doll figures, they have since been unanimously dismissed from this role by scholars and firmly established as having a purely religious significance. They represented in fact the Egyptian workers who were buried with their masters, to serve him in the life after death, as they had served him before it. The placing of these ritual figures exempted the real slaves from interment, so that the *Ushabti,* if not children's playthings, were at least symbols of early humanitarian feelings.

But are these scholarly arguments perhaps making too much of a simple childish instinct? Obviously early dolls are not to be confused with prehistoric idols, ancestor images, or fetishes. Many of these talisman figures were connected with birth and fertility, like the Maori *tiki* which was worn round the neck to ensure an easy birth or a handsomely large family. Others were safeguards like the small bone figures which the Eskimos still fasten to their kayaks to preserve them from disaster. Others were designed to do harm, like the notorious wax figures in the likeness of the victim, which were then pricked with pins, or melted to extinction in the ritual fire.

Every child is born with a natural instinct to play: and little girls are born with a natural instinct towards motherhood. Poor children of all ages have always fashioned playthings out of the most wretched materials, without the encouragement of seeing them in expensive shops [figure 2]. Any woman left alone to amuse a baby may find herself making a primitive toy out of a

2 A rough wooden doll from Thebes, Egypt, dating from about 2000 BC.

5

3 A painted wooden Egyptian doll, with a Negro's head, about 2000 BC.

4 A composite doll on a corn-cob foundation, eight inches high, made by the Xhosa tribe at Tsolo, East Griqualand. South Africa.

handkerchief or a rag or a piece of paper. Therefore, although in the past too many fetishist figures in museums have been labelled as dolls in error, nevertheless the plaything in a crude form must surely have been an accompaniment of childhood from the earliest years.

Naturally such crude types of doll would not have survived the passing of time: the modern doll of far stronger construction often does not survive the rough passage of an average child's affection lavished on it for ten or twelve years. Many of the most exquisite examples of dolls in museums or private collections today have been preserved in their unnatural elegance owing to some accident of careful handling, or early rescue from the stresses of nursery life. Others show quite conspicuously the strain imposed by the average child on the object of its affection! It is natural to suppose, then, that the very earliest doll playthings have vanished for the same reason as prehistoric clothing has not survived to our own times.

Some scholars, supporting the idea of the natural place of the doll in a child's life, have advanced the theory that the religious figures, as they lost their significance, were handed over as toys to children. This is certainly a plausible notion, for why should not the same figurine serve many different purposes, in the same way as a child will now play with an ornamental figure on its mother's table or the children of the eighteenth century pounced on their mothers' discarded fashion dolls?

It is indeed impossible to overestimate the part which fantasy plays in the mind of the average child. The child who plays with a doll transfers something of itself into the elaborate game of make-believe which it constructs round the toy in its own mind. We find the same use of 'transference magic' in early religious rites, a rough figure being used in a number of rites involving the representation of a victim or a beneficiary. Is there a connection here between the fetishes of a religious ceremony and the doll figures of a child's ceremonial fantasy? It is interesting to notice that one explanation for the origin of the word 'doll' is a corruption of *eidolon*, the Greek for idol.

We know that the Hopi Indians used to give their cult images to children to play with at the end of their ceremonies [figure 17]. These were miniature dolls, exact replicas of the *katchinas*, the spirits of earth and sky impersonated by masked and painted Indians wearing fantastic feathered head-dresses. There were many hundreds of these *katchina* figures, representing the sun god, gods of the warm wind and soft rain, gods of the rainbow and Milky Way, and other denizens of the Indian universe, each with their corresponding doll figure made of dry cotton-wood root and brilliantly painted. The children were probably presented with the *katchina* figures to teach them the details of their religion, in the same way as a Christian child

6

5 A Peruvian grave-doll of about 1500. It has been debated whether these figures, found in children's graves, are of religious significance or true dolls.

6 An English pestle, or 'champing-tree' for mashing fodder, of about 1800, made an excellent doll on account of its human shape.

today might be allowed to play with the figures from a crib after the Christmas season is over and forgotten.

It seems, therefore, in the words of Max von Boehm, the great authority on early dolls and puppets, that 'the genesis of the doll is to be found in a quality shared by primitive races and children', the ability to discern human and animal forms in all sorts of freaks of nature, including rocks and horns, bones and roots, all of which have stimulated the unsophisticated imagination.

Let us distinguish then between figures which were unquestionably not playthings, but were merely part of burial rites or other religious ceremonies, and other figures which have survived and may have had at times a twofold significance both as talismans and toys. In this sense, toy dolls are to be met with fairly freely among the various civilized races of antiquity. Among the extraordinarily rich amount of figures left behind by the Egyptians, there are certainly some, unlike the *Ushabti*, which are conceivably dolls [figure 3], and as civilizations advance nearer to our own, it becomes easier to trace definite doll play.

The dolls from ancient Greece are for the most part jointed [figure 9]: fashioned of burnt clay, with the limbs separately hooked on by string or cord, they have a real resemblance to the modern jointed doll. There are frequent references to the doll among Greek writers, including Demosthenes, and Plutarch himself tells a story of how his two-year old daughter Timoxena begged her nurse to give milk to her doll as well as to herself. A young Greek girl would dedicate her doll and its wardrobe to the goddess Artemis when she married at the age of twelve. According to Athenaeus, Sappho dedicated her doll to Aphrodite with these words: 'O Aphrodite, despise not my doll's little purple neckerchief. I, Sappho, dedicate this precious gift to you!'

In Roman times, toy dolls, made for the most part of clay, were also in common usage [figure 12]. The Latin word *pupus* or *pupa*, meaning a newborn child, has been adopted in many languages to denote the representation of a little child, including the German *Puppe* and the French *poupée*. The dolls of the rich were of a more elaborate nature. In the grave of a little girl in the Prati de Castello at Rome, a carved wooden doll was found which was two feet high and had movable limbs. The hands were carefully fashioned, but the arms and legs were represented only by smooth strips of wood. A beautifully ornamented little ivory doll was discovered in the sarcophagus of the Empress Maria, daughter of Stilicho and wife of the Emperor Honorius, who died in the fifth century.

The Roman girls, like their Greek predecessors, were wont to dedicate their dolls to a goddess on the eve of their marriage; and to prove that dolls at this time were no less dear to the little Christians than to the little pagans, we have the pathetic evidence

7

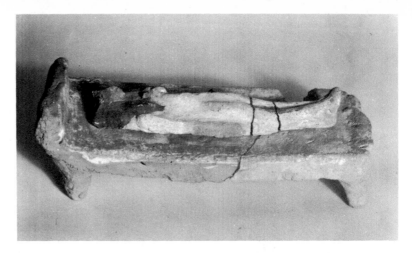

7 A traditional American corn-husk dolly.

of several examples found in children's graves in the catacombs.

Turning to the civilizations of the Far East, we find once again very early examples of dolls with a purely religious significance. In Chinese and Korean languages also, the word 'doll' came from the same root as the word for idol or fetish. But unlike the dolls of the Middle and Near East and Europe, these figures really do not seem to have co-existed as playthings. Gustav Schlegel, writing as late as the middle of the nineteenth century, observed that the little Chinese girls never played with dolls, because they were thought to possess magic powers. He believed that the idea of dolls as playthings was introduced to the Japanese by the Dutch.

Curiously enough, the Japanese doll festivals, whatever their significance, were always an important feature of the Japanese calendar. These two great festivals, that of the Girls on March 3, followed by that of the Boys on May 5, centre nowadays around a set of ceremonial dolls which every better-class family in Japan possesses, and hands down from generation to generation as an heirloom. These festivals have a known history of at least a thousand years, and beyond that their origins are shrouded in the mists of legends: what is certain is that their beginning had some sort of connection with an act of worship for the Emperor who was believed to have been of divine ancestry and the two most important dolls still represent the Emperor and Empress.

Illustrated in this book [figure 130] are some of the figures from a Japanese *Hina,* presented to a Western visitor to Japan in the 1880's: the gift was considered a great compliment, because the *Hina* as such was never commercialized for the Western market. The *Hina* at that date consisted of everything for the house and was given to well-to-do girls on their marriage, having a distinctly religious significance. Today Japanese dolls are made in millions to satisfy the demands of the tourist trade [figure 13]: but it is amusing to recall that even these stock souvenirs have their roots in the ancient and very un-Anglo-Saxon but hallowed custom of ancestor worship.

9 *(above left)* A Greek clay doll of the mid-fifth century BC, said to be from Athens.

10 *(above centre)* An Egyptian wooden doll of about 1000 BC.

11 *(above right)* An Egyptian pottery doll in the form of a captive, from about 2000 BC.

Turning to the West, and more especially the Far West, were there Indian dolls already in existence in America, before the white races discovered it? Scholars do not agree, but it is important to distinguish between dolls as the Indian tribes make them today [figure 14], showing strong traces of contact with our civilization, having native materials and workmanship but European form, and their original products which were definitely not fashioned with an eye on the tourist trade.

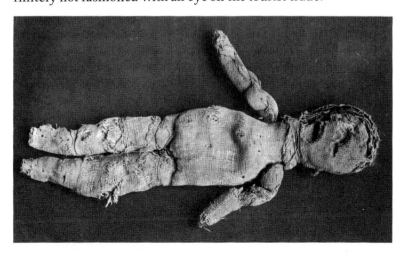

12   A rag-doll of the Roman period, from Egypt.

13 A Japanese geisha doll.

14 A doll dressed by Red Indians.

Clay dolls have been discovered in Mexico, marked with the insignia of the sun, belonging to the cults of the ancient Toltecs, supposed to date from the year 1000 BC. The present-day Indians of Mexico skilfully model little dolls of wax or put them together from rags or decorate them with flaxen ornaments; but they also cut out of paper dolls which are very close to the prehistoric 'board idols'. In ancient Peru, the rich civilization which flourished before the coming of the Spaniards, dolls were produced of a very high material standard [figure 5], including massive females in gold, and males in silver, both dressed in real cloth. The toys of the Peruvian children were interred in their graves when they died, and the dry earth contained so much saltpetre that not only these rich playthings, but also comparatively primitive ones of plaited straw, have come down to our times wonderfully preserved.

In the great continent of Africa, with its long history of magic and fetishism, it is not surprising to find that these elements are very strongly present in all their early dolls [figure 15]. Miss Alice K. Early quotes the example of a tribe in Africa today, in *English Dolls, Effigies and Puppets,* where dolls are still regarded very definitely as symbols of the occult: a missionary's wife who lived amongst them was so worried by the fact that none of the children played with dolls that she took the trouble to send for some modern dolls from England. But the moment the dolls were distributed among the children of the tribe, they vanished, and no trace of them was ever found, nor could she ever get any information about where they had gone. The little figures were considered to have dark powers which made them far too dangerous for children to handle!

We have seen how all these early dolls have two possible roles, as fetishes or playthings. They also fall into two forms, which anticipate the two main types of doll which will be discussed in this short work. The first is the sophisticated type of doll, of complicated design, where the head and other features are treated as separate entities, although the doll itself may be shaped out of a single unit [figure 22]. The second type consists of a solid single lump, which may be a broomstick or a clothes peg, but depends for its verisimilitude on having its features painted on from outside. Basically this is always the doll of the poor child: garishly painted, attractive and incredibly cheap, such a doll is still sold for a penny in the popular bazaars of India and Ceylon today. Both types are equally important in the development of the doll, for although more expense and workmanship may go into the making of a sophisticated doll, it is significant that doll collectors are often as fascinated by the very simple types they find in the course of their research, rightly recognizing that these cruder manifestations are of equal sociological value.

16 A Zanzibar doll made of millet stalks and dressed in fetishist beads and a Zanzibar jerkin, eight inches high.

15 Twin dolls of the Basuto tribe made of beadwork on a cartridge-case foundation, South Africa.

17 Three Hopi Indian dolls; the middle one, about three inches high, represents the thunder-god, and the others two lesser tribal deities.

The Wooden Doll

18 *(opposite)* A group of dolls from the Palladian dolls'-house at Uppark, Sussex, dating from about 1720. They consist of the master and mistress of the household and their children, surrounded by their servants.

19 Two early English wooden dolls, dated between 1720 and 1730, showing the typical almond-shaped eyes, thinly traced eyebrows, highly coloured cheeks and thin spatular hands.

THE EARLIEST RECORDS of European dolls are literary, rather than actual, and the mention of rag dolls *(simulacra de pannis)* in the *Judiculus Superstitionum* of the eighth or ninth century provides an explanation, for a rag doll would stand a poor chance of survival through the Dark Ages. The earliest dolls which have survived are actually made of clay: the soil of old Strasbourg revealed specimens dating from the thirteenth century, and clay dolls dating from the fourteenth century were discovered under the pavements of Nuremberg, including figures of children in swaddling clothes, monks, and ladies dressed in the medieval

20 An early German doll-maker at his trade. A woodcut from the *Hortus Sanitatis*, Mainz, 1491.

21 Another illustration from the *Hortus Sanitatis*, showing a fifteenth-century German doll-maker.

22 *(opposite)* An early jointed doll, believed to have belonged to Alicia Boleyn, cousin of Queen Anne Boleyn.

fashion of the times. A proper doll-maker is recorded as working at Nuremberg as early as 1413: and in the medieval *Hortus Sanitatis* we find an illustration of the doll-maker actually plying his trade [figures 20 and 21].

But we must look to the mention of *tocke* in early German writers to gain a true idea of the direction which early doll-making was to take. *Tocke* originally meant blocks of wood, and it is impossible to exaggerate the importance of wood as a material in those early days. What was more, the great source of wood lay in the German or mid-European forests, so that those craftsmen-in-wood who established Germany's early pre-eminence in the toy industry, found themselves with their material on their doorsteps. Many of the earliest examples of wooden dolls are scarcely more than rough blocks, while in the forefront of toy development, woodcuts show that the doll-makers of Nuremberg were already attempting dolls [figure 20] with movable limbs as early as the fifteenth century. Here we have an example of the most primitive aspect of toy-making, the instinct which leads a peasant sitting by his fire to fashion something to amuse his child out of an odd lump of wood, leading gradually to an extensive trade.

At the same time a fashion was springing up in different places all over Europe which involved a far more complicated and formal use of the material, and which if not precisely part of the main stream of doll development, at least led to an elaboration in methods of doll-making: this was the practice of the Christmas crèche. One legend has it that the idea of the crèche originated with St Francis of Assisi himself in Italy at the beginning of the thirteenth century. Certainly the saint made a special point of arranging Christmas festivals to illustrate as closely as possible the happenings at Bethlehem, in order to bring home the human nature of the Christmas message to the people among whom he lived. It would be an attractive notion to think that this charming custom actually originated with one of the most appealing saints in the calendar. But the custom of the Christmas crib is in fact far older – as old as the tradition of celebrating Christmas itself, which was first established by Pope Liberius in 354. Sermons by St John Chrysostom and St Gregory Thaumaturgus in about the year 400 make references to the existence of a crib with figures of the Holy Family, and even the now hallowed ox and ass.

Nevertheless, once established, it was in Italy that the crib became chiefly popular, which may account for the persistence of the legend about St Francis. The dramatic, colourful yet at times childlike nature of the Italians obviously finds something very satisfying in the cult of the crib. It was in Naples and the south, moreover, that the crib found its highest artistic form: in 1478 there is a record of a certain Jaconello Pepe giving a commission to two sculptors, Pietro and Giovanni Alamanno, to make

23 An Italian nativity group, mainly Neapolitan in origin, and dating from the early nineteenth century.

24 *(opposite)* An early wooden doll with a carved and painted head, wooden body and jointed legs. It dates from 1690, and is said to have been given by the family of the Old Pretender, James Stuart, to the family of one of his supporters.

25 A woodcut of 1450, showing a young girl holding her doll and its cradle.

26 An early nineteenth-century wooden Dutch doll which operated a spinning-wheel.

a crib for his family chapel in S Giovanna a Carbonara. The individual pieces are listed as follows: the Virgin Mary, who is to wear a crown, St Joseph, the baby Jesus, eleven angels, two prophets, two sibyls, three shepherds, twelve sheep, two dogs, four trees, an ox and ass – very much what you might expect to find in a modern crib scene. By the sixteenth century the crib had crossed the Alps, and the inventory of a Carmelite monastery in Bruges in 1537 mentions the existence of two of them. By the seventeenth century the Jesuits had introduced them to Munich, where the crib found an immediate popularity with the home-loving, religious-minded Bavarians. From now on, crib scenes were to play a very important part in the lives of peasants throughout Italy, Austria and Germany. Some of the scenes, indeed, provide an elaborate commentary on the daily life of the villages of the day: for they include merchants and their shops, carpenters, musicians and smiths, generally carved out of wood and prolific in informative and interesting detail.

Other crib scenes were of a grander quality, and were often added to year after year by their makers [figure 23]. In some convents nuns would spend the whole year dressing the dolls in anticipation of Christmas, as a sacred duty, and by the eighteenth century Neapolitan crib figures were said to rival queens and empresses in the richness of their clothing. Families would visit their neighbours' cribs on Christmas Day, vying with each other in the splendour of their efforts, while King Charles III of Naples actually made cribs with his own hands, and persuaded his queen to make the dresses.

All those who visited Naples at this period, including Goethe, commented upon the splendour of the cribs, and as the years passed, the complication of the background, incorporating automatic dolls as well as richly dressed ones, was such that one feels that the original simple Christmas message of St Francis must have been somewhat obscured in the elaboration of detail. One turns with relief to the notion of the Bavarian peasants, carving their own figures throughout the winter nights and retaining, surely, a more devout attitude to the whole custom.

Returning from this by-way to the main course of doll history, we find important advances all over Europe in the sixteenth century, not only in Germany. In France, for example, there are records of dolls being offered for sale among other luxuries on the stalls of the *Palais de Justice* as early as the middle of the preceding century: in a contemporary description of the Parisian scene, Antoine Astereau calls them 'charming and attractively dressed'.

By 1530 the Emperor Charles V was prepared to pay ten francs – a large sum in those days – for dolls from Paris for his little daughter, in spite of his professed hatred of France. King Henry II had six dolls sent from Paris to his daughter for the

27 A seventeenth-century English Puritan doll, about nine inches high, carved in oak. Her deep collar and plain dress illustrate the severity of the Puritan costume.

sum of nine francs, and in 1571 the Duchess Claudia of Lorraine sent for six of the most beautifully dressed dolls in Paris, to be presented to her newborn grand-daughter, the Duchess of Bavaria. But whereas the clothes of these dolls were probably elaborate and fashionable in the current ladies' style, the bodies were still fairly primitive, consisting either of a bundle of rags, or a leather bag filled with bran or sawdust. The legs of these dolls were frequently omitted altogether, as unnecessary under a long full skirt, and the whole body rested on a hoop petticoat.

At the same time the dolls of the poor continued to be made uncompromisingly of wood, and it was these wooden toys which started to travel freely outside their native land. They were made in great quantities in Germany, and once released from the hands of the craftsmen, would be bundled up in dozens by the salesmen who toured Europe with them.

As early as 1585 Sir Walter Raleigh took gifts of wooden dolls to the English children in Virginia. Certainly by the seventeenth and eighteenth centuries simple wooden dolls of the type we would now call Dutch dolls [figure 26] were being imported into England in large quantities from the Netherlands, to whom the craft for fashioning very simple, very cheap wooden dolls had spread from Germany; hence the adage of the English nursery:

The children of England take pleasure in breaking
What the children of Holland take pleasure in making.

These early Dutch dolls were in fact known as 'Flanders babies', but it is extraordinary how little the type varies from

19

29 A very early English wooden stump doll of about 1600, showing the traditional doll-shape in its most rudimentary form.

30 An eighteenth-century Italian child doll made of composition over wood, just over two feet high.

31 An interesting early eighteenth-century American wooden doll from Pennsylvania, nine-and-a-half inches high, crudely carved from a pine-post, and painted a greenish-grey colour with black and red dots.

32 A rare Parian boy doll in its original eighteenth-century French costume. The head, hands and legs are all extremely finely modelled.

33 and 34 A seventeenth-century doll representing a Dutch kitchen-maid, and a detail of her elaborate hair-style.

the simple German doll made by a Sonneburg toy-maker in the sixteenth century, to an eighteenth-century English 'Flanders baby', to a nineteenth-century Dutch doll, of the sort Queen Victoria used as a basis for her own vast collection, down to the little roughly made Dutch dolls which one can still buy in doll shops today [figure 36].

By the time Princess Victoria came to make her famous collection of dolls, wax, composition and parian dolls were far more popular in England than the old-fashioned wooden doll, and it is interesting to speculate what led the fourteen-year-old Princess to choose this material for what is perhaps the most famous collection of costume dolls in the world. There are 132 of them [figure 50], of which thirty-two were actually dressed by the Princess herself, and the rest by her governess, the Baroness Lehzen. Nearly all represent famous artists of her favourite operas and ballets dressed for one of their favourite roles on the stage, but some represent court ladies such as Juno, Countess of Durham, or Mary, Lady Roxburgh, or the Duchess of Worcester. They are between three and nine inches tall, and have the traditional sharp little wooden noses and vermilion cheeks of the Dutch doll, although the severity of the black-painted hair is relieved by clusters of black ringlets on each side. The costumes, in contrast to the stiff wooden figures, are made of the most exquisite gauzy materials in fairy-like pastel colours. The ballerina, Mlle Proche, wears a white silk costume trimmed with scarlet ribbons, and is presented as she appeared in the ballet *La Sonnambula*. This we learn from the *List of my dolls*, the detailed catalogue which Queen Victoria herself kept in a copy book in her own handwriting. In this is given the name of each

35 Sally, the 'White House doll', so called because she was the property of Mary Louisa Adams (grand-daughter of President John Quincy Adams) who was born at the White House in 1828.

22

36 A group of traditional Dutch dolls, dressed as Oxford undergraduates and dons by Miss Rhoda Davenport at the end of the nineteenth century.

doll, who dressed it, and what character it represents.

Not all the dolls are ladies: there are about eight gentlemen in the whole collection, including a dancer dressed as Robert, Earl of Leicester, from the ballet *Kenilworth* which the Princess saw performed in 1831 when she was twelve. Queen Elizabeth I, who features in the same ballet, is sumptuously dressed, but nevertheless the Princess Victoria did not approve of Elizabeth: 'She cut off the head of my ancestress, Mary Queen of Scots'.

Queen Victoria's dolls certainly crowned the history of the simple wooden doll with splendour, and are today well worth a visit in the London Museum where they are shown, the Museum itself being housed in part of Kensington Palace where the young Victoria spent her girlhood.

The earliest American dolls, which the children of the first settlers played with, were also of this simple wooden type, for except for rag dolls, there was nothing else available to them [figure 31]. Pioneer fathers, although not originating from a peasant class, whittled them for their children, in exactly the same way as Bavarian peasants on the other side of the world, for like the Bavarians, they were largely dependent on wood for their necessities of life.

These early American 'Pennywoods' or 'Peg-dolls' – the name being the American equivalent to the English 'Flanders baby' or Dutch doll – were not always crude and unadorned. An old wooden doll in an American collection has two corkscrew curls carved down the sides of its face, and an interesting wooden doll in the Annapolis collection of Miss Alma Robeck is a Negro boy with pearl buttons for eyes and set-in teeth, made of chestnut

23

37 'Old Susan', a doll which dates back to the eighteenth century, and was brought to America from England in 1773. Her brown eyes are made of real glass, and her hair is human hair. Her wooden head is covered with gesso.

38 A French Fashion doll with Parian head, hands and feet, and a cloth body. She wears an old Russian court-dress, dated about 1810.

39 *(opposite)* A doll which is reputed to have been dressed by Marie Antoinette while she was imprisoned in the Tuileries.

24

wood, jointed at shoulders, hips and knees. Others have the bright red painted cheeks which have led some over-made-up ladies to be described as looking like Dutch dolls.

Not all early English wooden dolls, however, were of the simple Dutch doll type. As wood continued to be the staple material of the doll industry and was not really superseded by wax and other new materials until the nineteenth century, some examples of early English dolls, made of wood or partly of wood in a more elegant style, have survived to our times. The earliest dressed wooden doll in the Victoria and Albert Museum of London dates from about 1690 [figure 24], and is said to have been given by the family of the Old Pretender, James Stuart, to one of their loyalist supporters as 'lately in use in Holyrood House'. She has the large head, painted eyes and outsize, somewhat scoop-like, hands, typical of English dolls of this date, compared to the slightly later 'Queen Anne' type, as it is known to collectors. This had white glass eyes and black pupils, lathe-turned body and peg-jointed limbs, and having once appeared as a type, it was to persist for the next seventy years.

A disproportionately large head was certainly one of the characteristics of the English wooden doll, at any rate in the seventeenth and early eighteenth centuries. This, and the tendency to colour the cheeks highly, give these English treasures a rather sinister appearance [figure 37]. To use once more the human comparison, the wooden dolls of the time of Queen Anne, some fine examples of which are in the Victoria and Albert Museum, have faces which could remind one of macabre old ladies, whereas the Dutch dolls look more like bedizened young girls.

Wood was now used in combination with other materials. Whereas the early English doll of the time of James I had been pine wood and cone-shaped, looking rather like a skittle [figure 29], by the time of Queen Anne, many dolls have arms and hands of yellow kid attached to the wood. Others, which are still made entirely of wood, have their heads, shoulders, forearms and lower legs painted, and sometimes a thin layer of composition gives a glossy surface to the paint. Movable arms were contrived by piercing the shoulder, and passing through this hole a little wooden shaft to which arms were attached, so that they could be raised, lowered or turned in a circular movement. Elbow joints, and jaws at the hip, knee and ankle, later followed the same pattern [figure 40].

Eyes were mainly painted with well-marked eyelashes and delicate, rather Oriental, eyebrows, although fixed glass eyes were also found occasionally in wooden dolls as early as the reign of Charles II. There is in fact no definite clue to the date of the first pair of glass eyes, and conversely it is dangerous to use the eyes alone to date any particular early doll, because of the lack of

40 A wooden jointed doll made between 1740 and 1760. Her excellent condition suggests that she must have been put away carefully.

certainty about the subject. The early glass eyes do not have pupils, but are made of blown glass with the dark colour inserted afterwards [figure 37]. The early eyes are also generally brown, and brown remained the favourite colour for dolls' eyes until the accession of Queen Victoria brought a patriotic wave of blue-eyed dolls. From then onwards blue displaced brown as the favourite colour and today, at any rate among the dolls of the English-speaking world, it is still the doll with eyes of Hanoverian blue which is most popular.

As the eighteenth century passes, the costumes of the dolls become more elaborate, even if the same traditional moulding for the body may be used over a number of years. The details of the dolls' clothing, their vests, petticoats, hair-style, panniers, and necklines, and the whole trousseau with which a doll might be surrounded, provide us with valuable information on the fashions of the century, quite apart from their interest as actual dolls. In 1776 a Miss Delaney wrote wryly concerning a doll she had dressed for a young friend of hers: 'Miss Dolly's mode box just packed up containing a lady *à la mode* in accoutrements – but in every other respects *tout au contraire*, for she can neither rouge, giggle nor run away.'

The doll to which she referred was intended simply as a plaything. But dolls did also play a very important conscious role in the history of fashion quite apart from their unconscious one, as we shall see in the following chapter on the actual Fashion dolls.

41 A family of six wooden dolls of traditional Dutch doll type, from the second half of the nineteenth century. They have pointed wooden noses, painted cheeks and black painted hair, parted in the middle.

Fashion Dolls and Pedlars

42 *(opposite)* A French 'Pandora' doll of about 1770.

THE HISTORY OF THE FASHION DOLLS was at first closely bound up with that of France. It confirms the natural pre-eminence of Paris in the world of fashion to find an English Queen sending over for the latest French styles as early as the fourteenth century, presumably unsatisfied by the products of her native country. For the Fashion doll was the earliest method of illustrating for foreigners the current mode in full and copyable detail – a role later filled by the prettily designed fashion plate, and still later by the glossy fashion magazine. The Fashion doll makes its first appearance long before such mechanical means of reproduction as the woodcut and the copperplate. The immense detail of its

43 Three Pedlar dolls with *papier-mâché* heads and hand-sewn white kid bodies with wooden limbs. The centre doll dates from 1830, and the smaller pair were made by Jesse Cross in 1870.

44 An eighteenth-century French Fashion doll wearing an embroidered dress trimmed with gold lace.

45 A French Fashion doll dressed by the couturier, Lanvin.

attire was the most convenient form of conveying correctly the latest vagaries of dress, word-of-mouth being notoriously unreliable and vague.

What were the early Fashion dolls like? There are a number of literary references to provide us with clues. In 1396 there is a record of Robert de Varennes, the court tailor of Charles VI, receiving 450 francs for a doll's wardrobe which he had executed, to be sent by Queen Isabeau of Bavaria to the Queen of England. As this was a considerable sum for those days, it is to be assumed that the dolls were life-size dummies, made to the measurements of the English Queen. Again in 1496 we find Queen Anne of Brittany ordering a large doll to be dressed for the Spanish Queen Isabella the Catholic, who was famous for the attention which she lavished on her dress. So high were her standards considered to be, in fact, that the doll was dressed twice over, in an effort to satisfy her.

When Henry IV of France was about to marry Marie de Medici as his second wife, he sent her several model dolls 'as samples of our fashions', presumably to impress her with the desirability of life at the French court. From all this we can conclude that early Fashion dolls were on a larger scale and more richly dressed than the ordinary play-dolls of the same period.

The great age of the Fashion doll, however, was the eighteenth century, when European travel became freer, and numerous small continental courts sprang up and flourished, with consequent demands upon the wardrobes of their great ladies. It became the fashion for ladies to own a pair of dolls, one dressed *en grande toilette,* and the other *en déshabille.* These were known as the *Grande Pandore* and the *Petite Pandore* respectively [figure 42], and were the subject of every extravagant whim of stylish dressing: hats, dresses, shoes, elaborate hair-styles and a great deal of miniature beads and jewellery.

What began as an aristocratic whim developed into an important part of the high fashion trade of the seventeenth century. These Pandoras were sent out by French fashion houses to England, Germany, Spain and Italy [figure 44], sometimes to exhibit the details of their dress, and sometimes for the details of their coiffure alone – as in a doll which Madame de Sévigné sent to her daughter, or the thirty coiffured dolls which were exhibited at the annual show of Saint-Ovide in 1763.

The importance of the Parisian Fashion doll as far away as Venice is illustrated by the fact that at the Sensa, the fourteen-day fair in the Piazza San Marco, a doll was annually exhibited clad in the latest fashion from France, and for the next twelve months this was sedulously copied by local dressmakers as the current style, until the next little ambassadress arrived to supersede it.

Nevertheless it was always with England that the main French fashion trade was exchanged, even during the War of the Spanish

Succession, when the hostilities between the two countries might have been expected to hinder such frivolous interchanges. The Abbé Prévost, writing in 1704 at the height of the war, observed: 'By an act of gallantry which is worthy of being noted in the chronicles of history for the benefit of the ladies, the ministers of both courts granted a special pass to the mannequin; that pass was always respected, and during the times of greatest enmity experienced on both sides the mannequin was the one object which remained unmolested.' And in 1712, when an embittered peace was still two years away, an announcement appeared in the English papers to the effect that 'last Saturday the French doll for the year 1712 arrived at my house in King Street, Covent Garden'.

There are frequent instances of Anglo-French co-operation in fashion throughout the eighteenth century. During the Regency, Dubois, the French Ambassador to London, later Cardinal Dubois, wrote to a Parisian dressmaker named Mademoiselle Filon, commissioning a large mannequin to show the ladies of London how the ladies of Paris were dressed, even down to the details of their underclothing. The answer was that a mannequin of this type would cost at least 300 francs, and Mademoiselle Filon would not risk the expense unless she was sure of being reimbursed. One imagines that the future Cardinal, rather than disappoint the ladies of the country to which he was then accredited, proceeded then to forward the money.

As their importance grew, the Pandoras came to be known as *poupées de la Rue de Saint-Honoré*, or even *les grands courriers de la mode*, under which title they were invoiced as having arrived at Dover in 1764. The usefulness of making the Pandoras life-size became apparent, for it was possible for customers not only to copy the clothes, but also to fit the actual dolls' clothes onto themselves, in rather the same way as model dresses today can be sometimes bought directly from French couturiers without fittings, after having been displayed for a season in the dress show.

In 1788 a Parisian milliner, Madame Eloffe, supplied one of her customers with a life-size doll in court dress. Rose Bertin, milliner and modiste to Queen Marie Antoinette, was commissioned to supply a doll for New Year's Day for Madame Dillon's little daughter, of which she has left us a full description in her account books: 'It was a big doll with springs, a well-made foot and a very good wig; a fine linen chemise; silk stockings and a long well-boned corset.' She also gave a list of the doll's ball dresses, her gowns of gauze and brocade, muslin and lace, and her caps and plumed hats.

Marie Antoinette herself used Rose Bertin to dress up dolls in the latest fashion for her sisters and her mother, the Empress Maria Theresa of Austria. Nor did the French Revolution put an

46 A French Fashion doll of about 1840 with a composition face and hands. She has an elaborate reticule over her wrist, and eyeglasses hang from a chain around her neck.

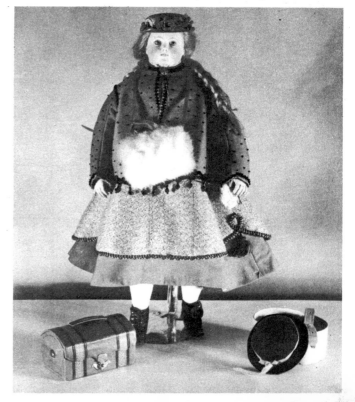

47 'Dolly Dimple' is typical of the Edwardian fashion for cut-out dolls. These could be dressed in several different outfits.

48 *(below left)* A wax doll of the 1870's in its original costume.

49 *(below right)* A doll representing a little girl made by Huret of Paris in 1867.

end to the fortunes of this illustrious modiste: she set up in business in London for a while, in order to serve her old clients among the émigrés, and her fashion dolls continued to circulate to the other European capitals, as far away even as St Petersburg.

The French Revolution had an indirect effect on the dressing of Fashion dolls – for by driving a number of aristocratic ladies to London as penniless émigrées, it inadvertently threw a labour force of skilled embroideresses upon the market. These ladies now supported themselves desperately with a craft which had once been used merely to while away an idle hour: and the result was a quantity of exquisitely hand-embroidered garments for the Fashion dolls of the time.

French Fashion dolls were not the only ones to adventure across water: throughout the eighteenth century, native English Fashion dolls also crossed the Atlantic to popularize English fashions in America, as we know from advertisements in the New York and Boston papers of the time. An advertisement in the *New England Weekly Journal* of July 12, 1733, reads: 'At Mrs Hannah Teats, dressmaker at the top of Summer Street, Boston, is to be seen a mannequin in the latest fashion, with articles of dress, night-dresses and everything pertaining to woman's attire. It has been brought from London by Captain White. Ladies who choose to see it may come or send for it. It is always ready to serve you. If you come, it will cost you two shillings, but if you send for it, seven shillings.' In 1796 Sally

50 Three dolls from Queen Victoria's own collection which she dressed herself as a child with the help of her governess, Baroness Lehzen.

McKean wrote to her friend Dolly Madison: 'Yesterday I went to see a mannequin which has just come from England to give us an idea of the latest fashions.'

It was the English who invented in 1790 a new type of Fashion doll, whose popularity was to last right through the nineteenth century, and is still in demand as a plaything for little girls. This was the flat card or stiffened paper doll figure, onto which could be attached a series of different dresses. At first they were made about eight inches high, and sold at around three shillings, which obviously made them a considerably more economical method of giving details of fashions than an elaborate life-sized doll figure which was difficult to transport over long distances. They were in fact akin to the pop-up books and panoramas and paper toy theatres so popular at the time.

33

51 *(above left)* A Fashion doll in late seventeenth-century dress. Her elaborate 'Fontange' coiffure makes her about twelve inches high.

52 *(above centre)* A German wax doll of about 1905, dressed in beige lace and tulle, and wearing an elaborate hat trimmed with pink flowers.

53 *(above right)* A late eighteenth-century English fortune-telling doll. She has a wooden head with painted hair and features, and jointed wooden arms. Her skirt is made of varicoloured folded papers on which the fortunes are written in ink.

Although the Germans had already used printed fashion plates, intended to be cut out, as early as the seventeenth century, the English cardboard figures combined the function of a doll with that of a fashion display [figure 47], as the many charming examples of this art illustrate. These cut-out dolls were particularly popular in Edwardian times when well-known actresses were often depicted, and even today there are large-size and magnificent cut-out dolls of this type on sale in the New York toy shops. Many of us, thinking of paper dolls, will always recall the melancholy love song of the 1920's: 'I'm going to buy a paper doll to call my own…'

The quantity of Fashion dolls certainly showed no signs of abating throughout the nineteenth century, and American collections in particular are rich in examples of delightful French bisques of the second half of the century [figure 56]. These were originally Fashion dolls and numerous milliner's models which used the new material of *papier mâché* to demonstrate the twists and turns of the new head styles. Franco-American co-operation was sometimes upset as when suspicions were aroused that the French were unloading old fashions in the New World, by means of outdated fashion dolls, but on the whole enthusiasm for the arrival of the visitors from France was great, and each new arrival was greeted with passionate attention. When they had served their fashion purpose, many of them found their way into nurseries as playthings. Others were carefully preserved under glass cases, so that whole conversation pieces of Fashion dolls are sometimes to be found in European and American museums.

But although the nineteenth century was a time when the Fashion doll flourished in quantity, its historical importance was superseded in the middle of the century by the French fashion plate, now framed and hanging on so many walls, and having the same obvious advantages of easy travel as the English paper doll. The nineteenth century is more properly the era of the elaborate child's doll and famous doll-makers, although even as late as the twentieth century the Fashion doll still sometimes plays an intriguing role of its own – as when an oriental potentate commissions a trousseau for his harem, and a series of dolls to go travelling, from which the incarcerated ladies make their choice.

But before passing on to the time of great expansion in both the materials and techniques of doll-making, it would seem appropriate to mention another aspect of the doll as saleswoman – although on a far humbler level than the elegant Fashion doll. I refer to the widespread practice of making Pedlar dolls in the eighteenth century.

These Pedlars are nearly all dressed as old women of the period [figure 55]; men or young women are comparatively rare. The simplicity of their dress, which is properly working-class, contrasts with the richness of the Fashion doll's clothing, and makes them, in addition, a valuable illustration of what working people wore at the time. They are generally made of wood, although the introduction of wax dolls brought a few early nineteenth-century examples of wax Pedlars. The women wore cloaks and bonnets, and often had elaborate aprons, over which they held out their trays, containing a wide selection of miniature merchandise and sometimes mottoes as well. Often the name of the Pedlar and the date was written in ink on a piece of paper and pinned to the tray, just as the real-life pedlars of the time had to display their names on their licences-to-sell.

The making of Pedlar dolls in the eighteenth and early nineteenth centuries presumably filled the need to display the variety of knick-knacks then found in the shops, for every sort of miniature object is found on their trays from tiny toys to household goods. At the same time Pedlars, sometimes known as 'Notion Nannies', were a familiar sight in the English country-side. In an age of scattered villages and foot-travel, the pedlar

54   A fine example of a bisque-headed Jumeau doll with a fabric body and kid limbs, dated about 1875–80.

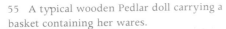

57 (opposite) A nineteenth-century French Fashion doll made by Huret.

56 A doll made in the 1860's by Huret of Paris, with a bisque head and gutta-percha body. She is surrounded by a typical lady's wardrobe of the period.

55 A typical wooden Pedlar doll carrying a basket containing her wares.

provided a valuable link with the great world, and brought to the lonely housewives news and gossip as well as pots and pans and sewing things, and it is not surprising that in this, as in so many other ways, dolls should provide a reflection on the social customs of the day.

Akin to the pedlar, and providing another source of rural excitement, was the fortune-teller, who is the subject of a number of English wooden dolls of the period. Sometimes a Pedlar doll will have a number of fortune-telling mottoes on her tray. One fortune-telling doll revolves on a circular stand, and when she stops, her stick points down to her client's fortune, good or bad. Queen Victoria thought it necessary to have a fortune-telling doll in her collection, and although its dress is rather grander than that of the Pedlars, being made of silk, its full skirt is constructed of a series of folded cards, each one of which has a motto written on it in ink. Queen Victoria's mottoes were obviously intended to be typical of the sort which are found on these dolls: for example 'Happy and blest with the man you love best', 'You'll have a boy to bring you joy', 'Though you love true, he loves not you', and more adventurously, 'For love and war, you'll travel far'.

There is an interesting late English Pedlar doll in the collection of Mrs de Witt Clinton Cohen, New York, dressed as a veteran of the Crimean campaign, who displays his licence-to-peddle on his box: crippled veterans of this campaign were once familiar sights on the streets of London, and were given peddling licences, commemorated in this particular doll.

Proper Pedlar dolls are of course peculiarly English, although many have found their way into American collections. At the same time the Southern states of America had their own pictur-esque Negro pedlars, whose street cries were as colourful and famous as those of the English street-vendors in Queen Anne's London. A Negro flower-merchant of unknown origin, in a gaily sprigged dress with a black linen face, which turned up in Massachusetts from the stock of an old New York doll shop, while not of the same antiquity as an English Pedlar doll, is neverthe-less an intriguing commentary on this phase of American life.

Wax, Papier-Mâché and Composition

59 An English wax doll of about 1840 with kid hands and wearing a wig.

58 *(opposite)* Two Edwardian wax dolls in full evening dress.

(following spread)

60 *(left)* An English wax portrait-doll of Queen Victoria in her Coronation robes, about 1840.

61 *(right)* An early Montanari wax doll about twenty inches high, which is reputed to have been shown at the Crystal Palace Exhibition of 1851. She is seen with a souvenir box of that date.

THE POPULARITY OF THE WAX DOLL in Victorian England was largely due to the efforts of one woman, Augusta Montanari, founder of the Montanari family firm. But wax dolls were not new. They had in fact been known in England many years before the work of Augusta Montanari and her son Richard brought them into prominence from the Great Exhibition of 1851 onwards.

It is said that wax was used in Italy at a very early date for making religious figures, and wax was also used at an early date for funeral images in Europe. References to wax dolls, the products of Daniel Neuberger of Augsburg, 'so marvellously coloured that they seemed alive', are found in Germany as early as the seventeenth century, and wax heads were moulded with elaborate hair styles for the fashion designers in France in the eighteenth century. But the development of the wax doll, as such, was really the achievement of England [figure 59], where the wax-maker's art was directed towards the making of dolls in the eighteenth century, as the popularity of the play-doll increased, and old materials such as wood could no longer give a sufficiently attractive and artistic finish.

At first the use of wax poured into moulds resulted in a certain monotony in the heads produced. Head and shoulders only were made of wax [figure 86] and body and limbs were of some different material, either wood, stuffed calico or cloth, or kid. The use of wax for the hands was a later introduction, and the finest wax dolls, which have arms and legs also in wax, are of a still later date.

Gradually, however, the wax for the heads came to be treated in a more adventurous manner. The wax could either be solid and modelled, or melted and set in moulds, to form a shell by a series of thin layers, or used in a layer over some other material such as wood, metal or composition. Unfortunately the early 'ball-head' technique for inserting the hair into the scalp, by means of a slit cut into the top of it, resulted only too often in a series of long cracks running down the wax face and shoulders; a sadly large number of early wax dolls are disfigured in this manner. Wax dolls whose hair was also of wax, moulded in one with the head, although perhaps less appealing and lifelike, stood a better chance of coming down the years undamaged. These wax dolls with moulded hair, sometimes known as 'pumpkin' or 'squash-

head' dolls, as opposed to the 'ball-heads', were particularly popular in the 1840's, and considerable numbers of them have survived in museums and private collections.

In the early wax dolls, cheeks and lips were painted directly onto the surface, as were the eyebrows and eyelashes. I have already mentioned the early use of fixed glass eyes in English dolls. Moving eyes were first used in England in about 1825: the eyes now opened and shut by means of a wire coming out of the body at the waist line, easily concealed by the elaborate clothing worn by the dolls of the period. The later counter-balance system of shutting the eyes by a system of lead weights, used by most modern 'shut-eye' dolls, came in about 1870, and in the 1880's eyes moving from side to side were introduced, but they remained comparatively rare.

In all the early wax dolls, before the time of the Montanaris, the problem was to use the material in a lifelike and attractive manner, and many of the early wax dolls may fairly be considered to be dull in character compared to the quaintly appealing wooden dolls of the same period. The Montanari family changed all this [figure 91]. Certainly a genuine Montanari doll is one of the easiest types for a collector to spot, for the Montanaris brought a series of new techniques into wax doll-making which resulted in some of the most beautiful and lifelike dolls ever made.

The doll-making family of Montanari, about whom there has been some confusion, consisted of Madame Augusta Montanari, the mother who is listed in the London Post Office Directory in the 1850's as a 'model wax doll-manufacturer, of 13 Charles Street, Soho Square', and her son Richard Napoleon Montanari, who is listed in the Directories of 1870 under 'doll-makers (wax)' and whose name in the list bears the dagger indicating a wholesale doll-manufacturer. The husband of Augusta, Napoleon Montanari, appears in the same Directories as his wife under the same address but merely as 'Modeller', so that experts have now agreed that he was a modeller and sculptor in wax, rather than an actual doll-maker. Indeed the entries at the International Paris Exhibition of 1885 help to make the situation clear, for Augusta was given an award for wax dolls, and Richard exhibited wax dolls and dolls' heads, whereas Napoleon merely exhibited statuettes and figurines in wax.

The classic description of the work of Augusta Montanari occurs in Tallis' *History and Description of the Crystal Palace Exhibition of the World's Industry in 1851*, for it was at this Exhibition that her dolls first attracted public attention: 'The only exhibition of wax dolls that was deserving was one by Augusta Montanari, to which a prize medal was awarded. The display of this exhibitor was the most remarkable and beautiful collection of toys in the Great Exhibition. It consisted of a series

64 Three elaborately dressed dolls of the Edwardian period.

62 *(opposite above)* The groomsman from an Edwardian wedding group composed of wax dolls.

63 *(opposite below)* This doll with its china head and leather body was made by the well-known French firm of Bru. It has a characteristic heavy appearance compared with the more delicate Jumeau dolls. It stands about fifteen inches high and was made between 1875 and 1880.

of dolls representing all ages from infancy to womanhood, arranged in several family groups, with suitable and elegant model furniture. These dolls had the hair, eyelashes and eyelids separately inserted in the wax, and were, in other respects, modelled with lifelike truthfulness. Much skill was also evinced in the variety of expression which was given to these figures in regard of the ages and stations which they were intended to represent.' Tallis goes on to comment on the high price of the Montanari dolls – as much as five guineas undressed, and the dressed ones proportionately more expensive, a fact which is borne out by the comment of M. Henri d'Allemagne on the Paris World Exhibition of 1882: 'The wax dolls were of beautiful workmanship but their prices were prohibitive for general trade.'

Tallis draws attention to all the main features which distinguished the Montanaris from previous wax dolls. It is important to notice that the Montanaris used a new process for putting the hair on dolls' heads, by which each hair was placed individually in the wax [figure 87] – a labour which demanded

considerable skill and patience, and doubtless explained in part the expense of the dolls. *Harper's Bazaar* of 1877, in an article on the manufacture of dolls, wrote: 'The putting on of the hair… is an important consideration of the manufacturer, being the most costly part of the whole toy.' The article goes on to describe the method by which the individual hairs were inserted with a hot needle in the skulls of the expensive dolls, as opposed to the simple groove cut in the skulls of the cheaper ones.

The features of the dolls were characteristic of the type of beauty admired in mid-Victorian belles – small rosebud mouths, large eyes, generally blue and fringed with long dark lashes, and plump pink and white flesh on the arms and shoulders, moulded in dainty round curves [figure 91]. Great care was taken that their expressions should vary from doll to doll, by a droop of the mouth or the complexion of a cheek, which again differentiated them from their rather stiff-faced predecessors. Montanari dolls are not supposed to have any distinguishing marks, although at least one example has been found, now in a private collection in Louisville, Kentucky, with an 'M' incised on the inside of its shoulder, revealed when its head accidentally came off.

Tallis mentions that the prize-winning dolls were of all ages 'from infancy to womanhood'. Strange as it may seem, infant dolls were still something of a rarity at this date. Indeed it was the allure of the Montanari wax baby dolls which did much to popularize them [figure 67], although the earliest English baby dolls probably date from about twenty-five years earlier. It is true that some surviving eighteenth-century dolls are apparently of children, because their dresses have ribbons attached to them at the back, to indicate leading-reins. But the baby doll as such needed the craftmanship of Augusta Montanari to launch it in earnest. Her glowing lifelike wax first gave a universal appeal to the shape of a baby. It was in fact the Paris Exhibition of 1855 which first demonstrated the charms of the English-made baby doll to Europe, with such success that it was widely copied, particularly in Germany.

Why should the baby doll be such a comparative late-comer into the world of dolls? Early pictures of children with their dolls always show them holding what look like tiny adults in their arms [figure 73], while they themselves are dressed as miniatures of their parents. For of course the cult of the child and childhood, as such, has a short history. For the same reason that children were dressed like their parents, and were expected

65   Three fine examples of poupard dolls. The doll on the left is German of about 1908. Its head is mounted on a satinwood whistle handle with a squeaker. The centre doll was made by Jumeau in 1870 and is dressed as an oriental lady with a black wooden handle attached to a squeaker. The right-hand French doll of 1876 is dressed in satin and mounted on a white wooden handle attached to a musical box.

66 Two examples of modern American dolls, in which every effort has been made to imitate nature.

67 This Montanari wax baby doll was awarded a prize at the Crystal Palace Exhibition of 1851, and the gold-leaf stamp on her robe bears the inscription *A. Montanari, Exhibition Prize Medal, 1851, Class XXIX* encircling the profile heads of the Queen and Prince Albert.

as far as possible to conform to the same standards of behaviour, so the early dolls are all garbed in grown-up style, and their features are clearly intended to be adult too. Yet as the baby in any form has an immediate appeal to the future mother in any little girl, it is not surprising that the baby doll, once introduced, was extraordinarily popular, and has remained so down to the present day, many of the most beautiful of the modern dolls being in the form of babies with elaborate trousseaux [figure 66].

The Montanaris were not the only famous firm of wax doll-manufacturers, although their dolls are generally judged to be the finest. The Pierotti family also made wax dolls [figure 75], and their dolls were considered to have the most beautiful complexions, the wax being coloured by a secret process of their own. The cheeks were tinted, the corners of the eyes reddened, also the nostrils and the ears, and of course the mouth. The arms and legs were left the same colour throughout.

Pierotti dolls have extremely naturalistic curves and their necks are particularly effective, the necks of the baby dolls [figure 75] having a curve of flesh at the back. There are also lifelike creases at the wrists and ankles, and the little hands and feet have pretty dimples, with the nails indicated. The hairs were inserted in the scalp in small groups by a knife, instead of a hot needle, round and round the perimeter of the head until gradually the crown was reached. The bodies were generally of white calico, stitched carefully onto the wax head and shoulders, arms and legs.

The Pierotti family, like the Montanaris, were part wax doll-makers, part wax modellers, since the two trades were naturally allied. Doll-makers are traced in this family as early as the 1780's, when Domenico Pierotti first came to England from Italy: in 1854 Henry Pierotti is recorded as being a wax doll-maker, and in 1862 he was awarded a Bronze Medal at the International Exhibition for Wax Model Dolls, with inserted hair, while his daughter Celia exhibited foreign and English toys. The Pierotti family continued to supply the famous London toy shop of Hamley's with dolls up till 1930, a long history of co-operation; but although there are many fine authentic Pierotti dolls in private collections, like the Montanaris, they do not seem to be characterized by any particular signature.

Charles Marsh was another reliable English doll-maker whose works have attracted the attention of very many collectors. He made wax-over-*papier-mâché* dolls in London from 1870 onwards, and after his death his business was carried on until the 1900's by his widow Mary Anne. As there is nothing to show that Mary Anne Marsh did not continue to use her husband's old stamp 'Charles Marsh, London' after his death, it is as well to remember that dolls bearing this mark might have to be dated anywhere between 1870 and 1900. Charles Marsh's dolls have a

69 An Edwardian wax doll wearing a sealskin hat and painted china boots.

68 A wax portrait-doll of Prince Albert Edward, later King Edward VII.

(following spread)

70 *(left)* A monkey automaton doll of the Louis Philippe period. It nods its head and lifts the brass dome to disclose three dice which change their numbers. The musical box attached to it plays two tunes.

71 *(right)* A portrait-doll of about 1864 representing the famous Swedish singer, Jenny Lind. She has a china head and a soft sawdust-filled body.

peculiarly English air, with their long fair hair, generally set into the wax heads in rather thick groups of hairs, suggesting a vague parting in the centre. The mouths are painted pink, the nostrils are two red dots, and the eyes which are bright blue and inset, have inset eyelashes and eyebrows of real hair. His dolls tend to be slightly larger and plumper than the average wax doll: the limbs are of hollow wax, with two holes at the arm above the elbow, and two at the leg just above the knee. The hollow head and shoulders, all in one piece, are joined to the body by a thread passed through the two holes on the back and front, the body being stuffed and made of strong white linen.

A Charles Marsh doll in the London Museum bears the stamp on its chest in an oval: 'From E. Moody, Soho Bazaar. Chas. Marsh. Sole Manufacturer London. Dolls cleaned and repaired';

47

73 An illustration from a children's book of
verses by the celebrated Victorian illustrator,
Kate Greenaway, published in 1885.

72 A chef with a *papier-mâché* head and hair
made of animal wool.

and below it in a further oval the claim, 'Warranted to stand any
climate'. This was rather an optimistic assertion, for even the
most carefully made wax dolls were sadly subject to extremes of
heat, and rough wear of any sort. The thick wax of Montanari's
dolls was even more susceptible to bad conditions than dolls
made of wax over *papier-mâché*.

However, collectors can take comfort from the excellent
facilities for restoration of wax dolls which are now being
developed, especially in the United States, for the fact that high
pressure air travel can cause further ravages in the face of an
antique wax doll has increased the problem for American
collectors bringing old dolls back from Europe. Curiously
enough, the modern wax dolls, generally character dolls, now
made in Mexico by some secret process, are impervious to heat
and cold.

I have discussed in detail three of the best known English wax
doll-makers because the wax doll is generally agreed to be a
peculiarly English product, but of course wax doll-making
flourished in both France and Germany in the second half of the
nineteenth century. The French made thick wax heads similar
to the Montanari dolls. The German-made wax heads generally
had a thin coating of wax over a *papier-mâché* foundation and
Germany, in fact, ended by being the great source of the cheaper
wax dolls which were made there in large quantities.

Papier-mâché, while it came to be used underneath a thin
coating of wax for a number of dolls' heads, also had an inde-
pendent existence as a dolls' material [figure 77]. *Papier-mâché*
literally means chewed paper. As an invention, it is ascribed by
some to Italy and by some to France, in the eighteenth century,
while it is first traced in dolls' heads in Germany in about 1810.
Consisting of layers and layers of paper stuck together, it can be
modelled when wet, but dries completely hard.

Although the Germans took the lead in the making of *papier-
mâché*, a quantity of *papier-mâché* dolls' heads are to be found in
America, the work of the famous doll-maker Ludwig Greiner of
Philadelphia. Ludwig Greiner first patented them in 1858 and

74 A wax doll given by the Empress Farah of Persia to an International Doll Exhibition in Paris in 1962. It is covered with real pearls and has gold embroidery on its dress and veil.

75 A wax doll made by the famous doll-making firm of Pierotti. Their dolls were well known for their naturalistic expressions and life-like curves.

again in 1872, but as he was listed as a 'Toy man' in the Philadelphia Directory as early as 1840, and as there are certain pre-1858 *papier-mâché* heads in existence which bear the mark of his hand and the words 'Patent applied for', his work probably extended in America from the 1840's to the 1880's. He was a German immigrant, which possibly explains his mastery of the material, and the methods which he clearly set forth for us in his application for the patent, are those which he used:

'One pound of white paper when cooked, is beat fine, and then the water is pressed out, so as to leave it moist. To this add one pound of dry Spanish whiting, one pound of rye flour, and one ounce of glue. This is worked until it is well mixed. Then it is rolled out with a roller to the required thinness. After it is cut into pieces required for the mould, it is moulded. Wherever there is a part projecting out – for instance the nose – it must be filled with linen or muslin… What I claim as my invention and desire to secure by Letter Patent is strengthening the seams and projecting or exposed parts of dolls' heads by cementing or pasting on those parts, muslin, linen, silk or other equivalent material.'

So universally did Greiner carry out his claims concerning fabric reinforcements that Greiner dolls can easily be recognized simply by looking inside the head. The Greiner label is black and gold, but even when absent, the Greiner dolls, although varying in size and the colour of their eyes and hair, draw one's attention by their characteristically placid look which the American expert Mrs Eleanor St George described as 'dumb and stolid'. At the same time, they are so well made that many of them have come down to us in excellent condition, owing to their durable material and glaze, and only the noses are apt to be a little scuffed and battered. The Greiner bodies were generally home-made, and their arms and hands were of leather. The native German *papier-mâché* heads vary from Greiner's in that they have inset glass eyes, which Greiner did not use, and the *papier-mâché* is not as thick as Greiner's.

Similar to *papier-mâché,* and equally used underneath wax and enamel, was the material composition or 'compo' [figure 105]. It was made of a mixture of many materials such as plaster of Paris, bran, sawdust and glue, and although malleable when wet, it hardened into a durable form. It appears to have been pioneered in England and imitated later in Germany. The composition surface of the face would be brightly painted, and then waxed over, in order to give the proper mellow look to the complexion, so that like that of a pure wax doll, a compo doll's face was unfortunately liable to crack.

How sad it is that so many of the loveliest Victorian treasures have come down to us damaged, due to long use and the extreme fragility of the material: however, they are no less loved by

77 Two German *papier-mâché* dolls. The one on the left has blown-glass eyes and probably dates from 1845 although its costume is later. The doll on the right has painted eyes and dates from the 1830's.

76 A *papier-mâché* doll of the 1820's with a typical coiffure of the period.

78 *(opposite)* Two English wax dolls of the 1880's, dressed as children from the Greenwich Charity School, London.

collectors for their cracks and chips, and one is reminded of the song which the good fairy sang to her babies in Charles Kingsley's immortal story *The Water Babies*:

> *I once had a sweet little doll, dears,*
> *The prettiest doll in the world;*
> *Her cheeks were so red and so white, dears,*
> *And her hair was so charmingly curled;*
> *But I lost my poor little doll, dears,*
> *As I played in the heath one day…*
> *…Folk say she is terribly changed, dears,*
> *For her paint is all washed away,*
> *And her arm trodden off by the cows, dears,*
> *And her hair not the least bit curled;*
> *Yet for old sake's sake she is still, dears,*
> *The prettiest doll in the world.*

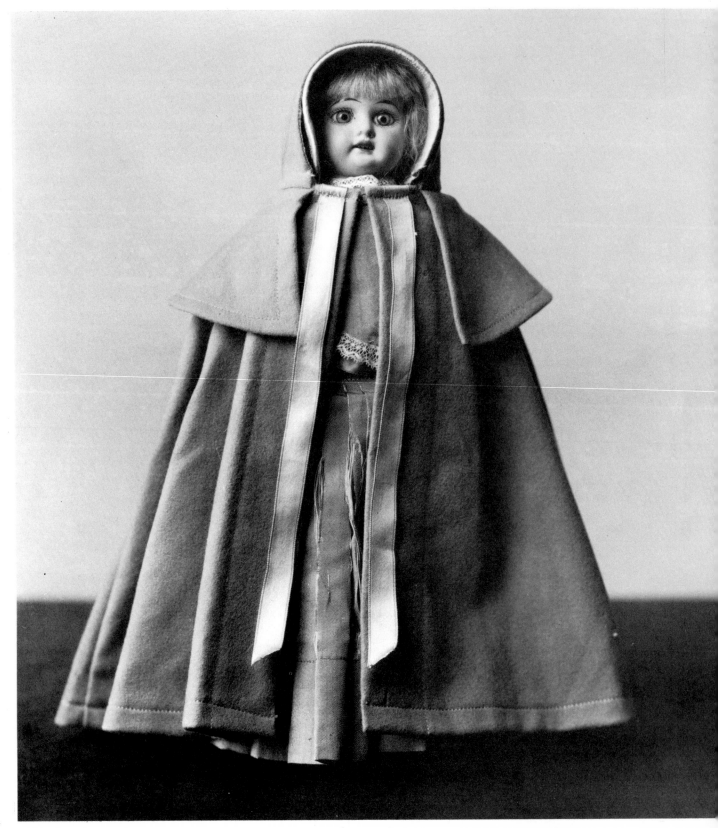

China, Parian and Bisque

80 An illustration from *Lieschens Puppenstube,* a German book for girls of 1884.

CHINA DOLLS' HEADS, and their many variations, including the so-called Parian and bisque ware, early attracted the attention of collectors. The nature of the material has often enabled them to be preserved in a miraculous state, compared to the more vulnerable wax, in the same way as many rare sets of china cups, plates and saucers have come down unharmed from the eighteenth century. For this very reason, perhaps, there have been more disagreements on the details of the history of china dolls' heads than in any other field of doll history, and there are more clashes of nomenclature from country to country.

As early as the fourteenth century, as we have seen, clay dolls were being made in Augsburg, Nuremberg and other places in Germany. Wherever there were suitable deposits of clay for making porcelain and china, dolls' heads were manufactured, the quality of the china depending not only on the quality of the clay, but also the fineness with which it had been ground. Early porcelain dolls are very rare, and few porcelain-head dolls survive from the eighteenth century, although figurines there are in quantity, and some prized dolls do exist from this period with the crossed blue swords of Meissen on their shoulder. The early German china heads are of a surprising variety of type, indicating probably that they were made in a number of different back yard kilns, because the German toy-making industry was always very much of a family affair.

During the nineteenth century china heads became extremely popular, and it is often difficult to tell early from late. Two clues worth following are that china heads with very steeply sloping shoulders are generally of an early date, and that the painted eyes of china heads in early models have a red line above them to denote the eyelid, whereas this is missing in the later and cheaper heads.

The hair-style of the individual head is often useful in dating it: that is to say, the middle parting and short close curls characteristic of the turn of the eighteenth century generally date a doll from between 1798–1805; later heads have the high back-swept topknot fashionable in the 1830's [figure 76], and the ear puffs which one associates with the early pictures of the young Queen Victoria; the waterfall or chignon hair-style is characteristic of the 1860's, and bangs of the 1890's, when they were much worn. But it is important not to strain the conclusions

79 *(opposite)* A nineteenth-century Shaker doll from New Lebanon, New York.

81 A fine German china head, dated 1840–50, with the characteristic black hair popular on china heads.

drawn from the hair-style too far when attempting to date dolls' heads, as the same head-mould was sometimes still in use after the hair-style had gone out of fashion.

It is interesting to find that whereas the eyes of china dolls are generally blue, with occasional deviations to brown, sometimes attractively executed in lustre, the colour of the hair is nearly always black [figure 81], with only very rare use of dark brown. As the Germans are a famously blonde nation, the artists were presumably enamoured of the striking contrast between the black china head and the white china face, which they preferred to the more anaemic appearance of a fair-haired china doll. However, a Los Angeles collector actually possesses a red-haired blue-hatted china doll – an extreme rarity. One type of china head was in fact produced without any hair moulding at all: this was the Biedermeier type of doll which had a black spot on its crown into which the doll's wig could be fixed with glue. There have been a number of arguments about the dating of these Biedermeier dolls, but now experts are inclined to agree on the 1830's, the Biedermeier period. The fact that these dolls often have the ankle boots without heels on their feet, which were characteristic of the period 1815–40, certainly supports this point of view.

Other china heads have an actual hole in the crown. German heads in particular favoured this, because it reduced the weight of the head, and as the export of china heads from Germany was an enormous business, it was an advantage to pay a lower tariff charge on a lighter head. Once arrived at its destination abroad, the hollow head could be closed up with cork or some other material, to which the wig could then be attached, its material varying from the fine hair of a real child, to yak's hair or mohair.

As china can be either 'hard paste' or 'soft paste' according to the elements in the clay, so dolls' heads are found in both varieties of texture. The white 'soft paste' heads usually show greater signs of wear than the pink heads, which being made of much harder paste, remain comparatively fresh in appearance.

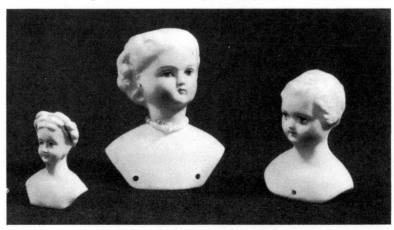

82 Three Parian heads dating from the 1860's. They show how this material lent itself to carefully modelled blonde hair.

56

83 A French Fashion doll
made of bisque with kid
hands, dated 1874.

It is these pink heads which were known in the past to collectors
as 'Chelsea' heads, but are now classed by some as 'pink lustre'.
  The term 'Parian' for dolls' heads has been another source of
confusion to collectors. How do Parian heads differ from bisque
heads? All unglazed china heads, whatever they are termed, are
in fact made of bisque, which is no more than a contraction of the
technical term for the 'biscuit' mix, which goes towards the 57

84 Two German bisque-headed dolls. The one in Highland costume is dated about 1890, and the one in Swedish costume is of 1877.

85 A bridal couple by Armand Marseille, made in Germany in about 1890. Both dolls have bisque heads and jointed leather bodies.

making of china, before it is dipped in its final glaze and fired. The fact is that certain unglazed and fired heads were produced without any colouring matter at all. These dead white heads came to be known as 'Parian' [figure 88] from their resemblance to the white marble from the Greek island of Paros, since they did have a superficial resemblance to marble statues. For the same reason the white unglazed dishes produced by Staffordshire potteries came to be termed 'Parian ware'. Heads with a moderate amount of colouring matter were known as 'blonde bisque', and highly coloured ones simply as 'bisque', while some rather coarse greyish heads were termed 'stone bisque'.

Fine early Parian heads were made at the Dresden potteries in Germany beginning in the 1850's and continuing through to the 1870's. The hardness of the paste made it possible to cast it in a mould of great detail and delicacy: the artists, particularly in the earlier models, were inspired to flights of imagination in the hair-styles, which incorporated braids, ringlets, plaits, curls and even wreaths of flowers and wheat in profusion [figure 82]. The eyes were generally painted in, although there are some rare Dresden heads with inserted glass eyes.

In contrast to china heads, however, Parian heads are generally blonde [figure 88], presumably because the golden colouring clearly went better with the dull Parian material just as black was shown up to greater advantage in the glazed china. Incidentally, Parian heads were sometimes made out of the same moulds as china and even wax heads.

It is out of bisque proper that many of the most beautiful dolls' heads in existence have been made: and the glory of bisque is largely due to the efforts of the Jumeau family firm who made the best and most famous of the bisque dolls between 1844 and 1898 [figure 54]. The Jumeaus are to bisque what the Montanaris were to wax. The early Jumeau dolls were imported from Germany and were actually 'blonde bisque' in type: this probably explains why the Jumeau dolls were not praised for themselves, but only for their exquisite gowns and undergarments at the Great Exhibition of 1851. In importing his dolls' heads, M. Jumeau, founder of the firm, was only following the fashion of the French doll-makers of the day. Nevertheless in 1862 he decided to strike out on his own, and free his firm from its German associations by undertaking the manufacture of his own dolls' heads, which he was determined should be infinitely more beautiful and artistic than the ever popular German ones. The new Jumeau heads were universally agreed to be of a rare beauty, distinguished among other things by their large, even oversized, soulful eyes [figure 128], which were made with enamel, exactly like artificial eyes for human beings.

At first the heads were made in one piece with the bust attached, but later M. Jumeau's eldest son invented a movable

86 A Fashion doll, about eighteen inches high, dating from 1877. She has a wax face and composition hands.

87 'Anne Fanny' is a family doll, about 35 inches tall. Her blue shoes were said to have been made for the Princess Royal in 1842 but did not fit her. Her hair and eyebrows were individually set into her head, and her eyes open and close.

swivel neck, possibly the first to appear in the doll world. This he patented in 1860. The heads of the Jumeau dolls were left open at the top, possibly in imitation of the dolls of German origin with which they started their business, and possibly also to make it easier to fix in the eyes. The dolls were made at the Jumeau factory at Montreuil in France in fourteen different sizes, the largest being about three feet three inches high, and each size was marked separately to distinguish it. The bodies of the early dolls were generally made of kid on a wire foundation; later wood was used, in a beautifully made body jointed at the waist, elbows and ankles as well as in the usual places.

This type of body, although a considerable carpentering achievement, was extremely expensive to produce in any quantity. When the Jumeau factory was fully established, a much cheaper form of composition body was assembled, each limb being cast in a separate mould, and the whole was joined together by the ball and hook method and copper wires. Jumeau's son is indeed credited with the invention of the composition body, strung together with elastic, a method which has continued up to the present day. The Jumeau composition bodies were painted at the factory, the hair was fixed to the head before it was joined to the neck, and the eyes, instead of being imported, were made in the same factory.

It is possible to find Jumeau bodies which are a combination of a number of materials: for example a kid-bodied doll with the upper third of the arms wood, the lower two-thirds bisque. Jumeau also made cheaper dolls with bisque heads fixed onto a simple stuffed cloth body, with leather feet. These dolls are generally far less richly dressed than their more elaborate sisters from the same workshop, and were obviously intended to appeal to a different market.

Encouraged no doubt by the success of the wax baby dolls, the Jumeaus also started to make bisque baby dolls on their own account [figure 92], and the Paris Exhibition of 1855 was marked by the success of their famous Bébés Jumeau, which were described as 'elegant and in good taste'. Another venture was the making of dolls with brown bisque faces to represent Negroes.

The characteristic mark, 'JUMEAU, Medaille d'Or, Paris', is apparently not found on Jumeau dolls before the advent of the composition body in the 1880's, and then it was generally placed on the body, only very occasionally on the head. Recognition of early Jumeau dolls depends therefore on their expression and countenance, rather than on any specific markings: in spite of this, their prettiness makes them amongst the easiest types to recognize.

The success, not only d'estime, but also financial, of the Jumeaus, induced other firms to enter the world of bisque dolls. Of these, the French firm of Bru is probably the best known, with

59

88 Two Parian dolls, of which the finely modelled Franciscan monk dates from 1800. The other doll is in Norwegian costume and has the blonde hair characteristic of Parian heads.

its characteristic shoulder-marking of the three letters BRU, one on top of the other. The Bru firm, however, never approached the Jumeaus either in artistry or in turnover: it is estimated that they were doing 200,000 francs of business at a time when the Jumeaus were grossing over a million francs. Bru dolls are highly coloured, and have slightly heavier faces than Jumeau dolls, being altogether more like the modern dolls in appearance. In 1898 the two firms of Jumeau and Bru joined together to form *La Société Française de Fabrication des Bébés et Jouets,* which explains why some dolls are found with the heads marked Jumeau and the bodies Bru, or vice versa, a fact which had puzzled collectors until the truth was published by Mrs Eleanor St George.

We have seen how the bisque doll was originally a German concept, and adapted by the French doll-makers into the famous French nineteenth-century *poupées de luxe*. At the same time, of course, the Germans continued to cast bisque heads in great quantities throughout the century, of which the finest type were the Royal Kaestner, dated about fifty years ago. Another well-known German doll-maker who made slightly cheaper dolls at the turn of the twentieth century was Armand Marseille [figure 85] who, like Jumeau, produced baby dolls of particular charm:

89 A French Jumeau bisque-headed doll, dated about 1880.

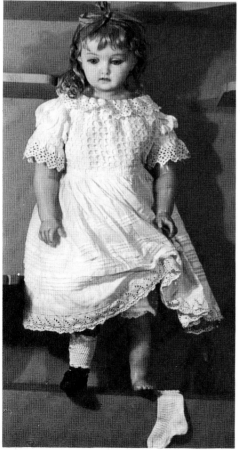

his dolls, which were marked by his initials and a number, usually on the back of the neck or just underneath the hair, are of sufficiently recent date to be coming into the hands of collectors from forgotten trunks in the attics of private houses. As any doll which came into England after 1890 had to be stamped with the country of its origin, many Armand Marseille dolls bear the words 'Made in Germany' in addition to their other marks.

Early Armand Marseille dolls had jointed kid bodies; by 1908 and 1909 their bodies were often of pink canvas with bisque lower arms, while the legs were simply stuffed to imitate black stockings. By 1911 there are many examples of dolls with wooden bodies, arms and legs, the arms and legs below the knee being covered with composition. Nearly all of them had eyes which open and shut, the eyelids being part of the eyeball, as in most dolls of this period.

The Armand Marseille dolls, although perhaps cheaper than the Jumeaus, are still dolls in the grand manner. But china and bisque were not used exclusively for dolls of splendid size and correspondingly high price. A whole different category of china and bisque dolls existed about forty to sixty years ago, called 'Frozen Charlottes'. These charming little dolls were anything from about four inches high, and strictly speaking should be made in one piece without any joints at all. They were bought by children with their pocket money, and their small size meant that clothes could easily be made for them by the children themselves out of scraps of material. They were the china and bisque equivalents of the wooden Pennywoods or Dutch dolls, and, as in the larger dolls, the china heads generally have black hair and the bisque heads blonde hair.

The name apparently derives from a Vermont folk ballad *The Fair Charlotte* in which the heroine persists in riding in a sleigh with her lover, inadequately clad, and as a result freezes to death at the end of the journey:

> *Fair Charlotte was a frozen corpse*
> *And her lips spake never more.*

Another name for them was 'Teacup dolls', on the grounds that they were small enough to stir the sugar in the ladies' afternoon tea and were given to the ladies at the end of a tea party as souvenirs; but this charming notion is rather discredited by the fact that some of them are at least twelve inches high, which would have made them rather clumsy teaspoons!

It would be impossible to conclude a chapter on china, Parian and bisque dolls without mentioning one aspect of the making of dolls' heads which has vexed many experts. This is the question of whether or not they were ever made in England, prior to the

90 *(opposite above)* An illustration to *Sing a Song of Sixpence* by Randolph Caldecott, which was published in 1880.

91 *(opposite below)* A wax Montanari doll of great beauty, about 27 inches high. Her body is made of white calico to which the wax arms, legs and bust are attached. She wears a dress which was worn by a four-year-old child of this period, about 1865.

93 *(below right)* A Victorian nursery. The doll's cradle lies empty on the floor as the little girl shows her mother her doll. From a series of plates in a story book of 1870.

92 *(below left)* A baby doll made by the famous Jumeau family. The eyelashes are clearly marked, and the intricate jointing of the body is well illustrated.

1914–18 war, which of necessity checked the flow of ready-made dolls' heads from Germany, and forced the English potteries to supply the deficiency to English doll-makers.

Alice K. Early discovered that Messrs Ridgways, Stoke-on-Trent, were very early manufacturers of porcelainous dolls' heads, and also of complete china dolls, some all of one piece, others with the shoulders and hips pierced with wires to give the arms and legs freedom of movement. From 1914 onwards numerous different types of china and porcelain dolls were produced in the potteries at several factories, and Ridgways may well have been producing dolls' heads as early as the middle of the nineteenth century. It would surely be extraordinary if such a flourishing area as the Potteries had not turned their attention to manufacturing dolls' heads among other profitable branches of china manufacture, before the Great War forced them to do so. This is, however, but conjecture, or common sense: it must be admitted that no documentary evidence of such an output exists on the authority of the Victoria and Albert Museum in London.

One may, however, fairly look at the famous Staffordshire figures, and wonder if their authors would not have naturally turned their hands from figurines to dolls, in view of the immense popularity of dolls as playthings in late nineteenth-century England.

Automata

95 A very early French walking doll of about 1826.

94 *(opposite)* A French automaton 'Rose Doll' of of about 1860, with a fine porcelain head and hands. Operated by clockwork, she rises from the heart of the rose, looks from side to side, and descends again into the rose which closes over her.

IN A CRAFT SUCH AS DOLL-MAKING, which takes infinite pains to imitate real life by art, it is natural that animation, the missing ingredient from even the most lifelike doll, should have provided important matter for study from the earliest years. From the collector's point of view, the eighteenth century undoubtedly furnishes the most exquisite examples of doll automata, while the nineteenth century was a time of ingenious invention, and the twentieth century in many respects merely copied the tricks of the previous century, or produced them as fresh discoveries.

But if the eighteenth century is the artistic peak of the automata, it certainly did not produce the earliest examples of them. The art of making automata was known as early as the third century BC and Petronius refers to a silver doll which could move like a human being. The Indian fairy-tale collection of Somdeva, which belongs to the eleventh century but includes material of an earlier date, mentions dolls moved by mechanism, of which one fetched a wreath, another water, a third danced and a fourth apparently even spoke out loud.

Research into the medieval and pre-medieval history of Europe reveals that moving images of one sort or another were constantly billed as novel attractions at fairs. As early as 1632 the town of Augsburg presented King Gustavus Adolphus with a splendid art-cabinet costing 6500 Reichsthalers into which the designer, Philip Hainhofer, placed a pair of mechanical dolls – a cavalier and his lady holding each other's hands ready to dance by means of an interior mechanism. Both are sumptuously dressed, with plentiful silver braid on their silken clothes, and may be fairly estimated as the best that Germany could provide in the way of dolls at this date.

In the early years of the eighteenth century a well-known Viennese preacher, Abraham a Santa Clara, spoke of 'dolls so ingeniously contrived that on being pulled, pressed or wound up they become animated and move by themselves as desired'; and Corvinus described in 1716 'the costly and ingenious dolls which display *actiones* by means of concealed clockwork', then the speciality of Augsburg and Nuremberg 'which are rapidly filling the world with them'. This type of movable doll, known as *la jolie catin*, was shown in the streets of French villages and towns by itinerant girl-sellers, and was illustrated as a familiar sight in the *Cris de Paris*.

97 An illustration from *The Land of Nod* by May Byron. The accompanying text reads, 'Then she'd a dream – and there was a dolly lovingly bending over her, stroking her face and hair'.

98 *Daisy and her Dolly*, an illustration from a Victorian scrapbook of 1895.

In the course of the eighteenth century several masters of the art of automata arose. First among them was Jacques de Vaucanson, whose automata, produced between 1738 and 1741, became world famous. They included a flute player with a repertoire of twelve tunes and a duck whose structure was anatomically entirely correct, and whose every bone executed its proper movements, as well as being able to quack in a most lifelike manner; moreover, when corn was thrown in front of it, it stretched out its neck, swallowed it, digested it by means of a chemical solution inside, and finally discharged it in true biological fashion!

Next came the family of Jaquet-Droz; the father, Pierre Jaquet-Droz, and his son, Henri. In 1760 Pierre Jaquet-Droz made a child doll, said to be capable of writing a letter of fifty words or so, called 'The Young Writer'; and in 1773, Henri Jaquet-Droz made two famous figures, one called 'The Designer', which could draw and is said to have sketched a portrait of Queen Marie Antoinette in her presence, the other called *'La Musicienne'*, which played a proper tune. The skill of the Jaquet-Droz family was such, and the mechanical toys which they made for the King of Spain were so fabulous, that they were in danger of being condemned as sorcerers by the Spanish Inquisition. They produced for him, amongst other toys, a sheep which bleated in a most lifelike manner, and a dog guarding a basket of fruit, which began to bark when any of the fruit was taken away from it.

A further skilled inventor was Wolfgang von Kempelen who made a speaking automaton in 1778, and a celebrated 'automatic' chess-player in 1769, against which Napoleon played a game of chess in 1809 and lost. Perhaps the chess-player should not properly be included among true automata, for its secret, which baffled observers, was to conceal a man inside the box on which it was mounted, who was able to watch the moves made by his opponent in a series of mirrors.

The flights of mechanical invention known at this time are indeed many and varied, and include such charming fancies as the automatic group made for Tippoo Sahib, the highly anglophobe Sultan of Mysore, which consisted of a life-sized tiger rushing to devour an Englishman in uniform! Although water, wind, mercury and clockwork were the only materials known to the designers, they made full use of them [figure 94], to the extent that even Italian and Austrian peasants, as we have seen in an earlier chapter, made automatic crib scenes where the background figures to the Holy Family could be seen tapping, hammering, buying and selling.

Italian artists of the eighteenth century produced particularly elaborate devices, which usually incorporated richly dressed dolls, for example a court lady seated at her dressing-table, with

99 An American walking doll about ten inches high. She has a bisque head and kid arms with a clockwork mechanism and key inside her skirt.

100 Four bride dolls of different periods. The two largest are English from about 1880 and have glass eyes and real hair. The third bride is probably French of about 1918, and is jointed at the waist in order to show off her clothes to their best advantage. The fourth doll is modern, and is made of Revlon plastic material in America and dressed by a Californian schoolgirl.

103 *(opposite)* A mechanical French doll of about 1860. She sits at her dressing-table, and when wound up, lifts her mirror and powder-puff and powders her face.

101 A drawing from *St Nicolas' Annual* of 1908.

102 A rare French doll of the time of the Second Empire, which actually swims.

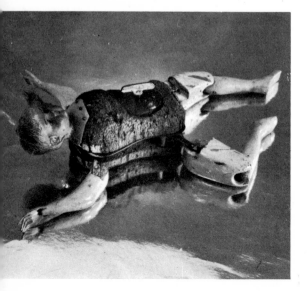

perhaps a Negro page in attendance. Negro servants are favourite figures in automatic groups or groups of musicians in control of a varied series of instruments [figure 108].

England was not entirely left out of the world of automata: she produced 'bristle' dolls in the eighteenth century: these were small harpsichord dolls, with a bunch of bristle or brush hidden under their long skirts. They would be placed on the harpsichord, and when the ladies tapped the keys, the vibrations caused them to dance. The same principle is still used in dolls today which 'dance' to the gramophone, and there is a modern American version called 'Microphone Sam', who tap-dances when any noise is made in front of the microphone.

England also provides examples of the famous type of 'tilting doll' which had originally come from China, where it was known as 'Stand up, little priest'. Tilting dolls were sometimes known as 'Fanny Royds'; there is a reference in the *Creevey Papers* to the unfortunate Queen Caroline, estranged wife of George IV: 'I had been taught to believe that she was as much improved in looks as in dignity of manners; it is therefore with much pain I am obliged to observe that the nearest resemblance I can recollect to this much injured princess is a toy which you used to call Fanny Royds.'

The Germans with their love of mechanical toys also retain their traditional skill at making them, while the French, and in particular the manufacturers of nineteenth-century Paris, produced marvellously luxurious mechanical dolls, which their buyers brought back to America and England with the same enthusiasm then, as modern collectors seize upon them now.

Often the celebrated doll-makers of the nineteenth century collaborated in the production of mechanical devices like a musical box. Jumeau dolls in particular are found on a great quantity of musical boxes [figure 70], the boxes being of Swiss or German origin, while the dolls are clearly French. One musical Jumeau doll in the collection of Mrs Grant J. Holt in the United States holds a bird cage in its hand, and when the music plays, the bird moves about in its cage, as if singing, while the doll's head moves from side to side and its free hand up and down. In this case, the musical box bears the label 'Jumeau', but often the characteristic Jumeau appearance, discussed in the previous chapter, makes musical Jumeau dolls as easy to recognize as ordinary ones. Another musical Jumeau in the Grant J. Holt collection is a boy doll, whose hand moves to and fro as the music plays, and puts a cigarette back and forward from his mouth, while his head tilts back as if smoking. Yet another delightful musical doll in the same collection is a little girl who teases a kitten at her feet with a piece of string with one hand and brings her doll to her face to kiss it with the other, all to the tune of *Ma Petite Bourgeoise*. A still later type of French musical doll, dating

104 A Negro conjuror made in France about 1860. When he is wound up, the conjuror lifts up his beakers and performs a series of tricks with coloured balls.

from the beginning of the twentieth century, would be mounted on a handle, and the music was played by twirling the doll round [figure 65].

But, of course, musical boxes and musical dolls are only one aspect of automata. The first speaking dolls made in any quantity were made in the 1820's by Johann Maelzel, the inventor of the metronome for the piano. A children's periodical, *Le Bon Génie,* reports that at the Exhibition of French Industry in 1823, there were dolls which said 'Maman' when their right hands were touched and 'Papa' when their left hands were touched, and Maelzel took out a patent for his invention in 1824. An advertisement of the time says: *'Pour six francs je remue les yeux et je tourne la tête. Pour dix francs je dis Papa et Maman.'*

Monsieur Bru, founder of the Bru firm, seems to have had a special penchant for mechanical things: in 1869 he took out a patent for perfecting the manufacture of dolls, having made a doll in 1867 which turned its head, showing two expressions. In 1872 his wife, Madame Bru, made what is described as a

72

105 A doll of painted composition, representing an American 'black mammy', dated about 1860.

106 An automaton piano-playing doll with a hand-operated musical box action. It was made in Germany about 1875 and has a porcelain head which moves as if reading the music while the hands pass over the keys.

107 The 'Autoperipatetikos' or clockwork walking doll made in New York in 1865 and patented there under this name.

'magical talking doll' which sang various different songs.

In 1887 or the next year, Thomas Edison, inventor of the phonograph, turned his attention to the problem of the speaking doll, and adapted a phonograph with round discs to go inside a doll. The result was a talking doll, whose remarks could be varied merely by changing the disc, like changing the record on a gramophone. These dolls were shown first at the Paris Exhibition and then at the Lennox Lyceum, New York City, and were described as follows: 'Twelve daintily dressed phonograph dolls standing in a row on a miniature theatre stage delighted fathers and mothers by repeating each, in turn, a verse from our well-beloved *Mother Goose*. The voices were high pitched, and taken together, rather monotonous. But the pleasure of a child who has one of these dolls promises to be endless, if he or she can restrain the instinct to find out where the voice comes from, for the firm who sells them will soon be able to put in the new phonograms with fresh verses, whenever the little owner desires a change.'

The *Société Française de Fabrication des Bébés et Jouets* also made a phonograph doll for the Paris Exhibition of 1900, but the making of it was apparently abandoned after the Exhibition, as although mechanically ingenious, it cost far too much to produce in any large quantities. For the same reason, no doubt, there is only one Edison phonograph doll which is known to exist; it belongs to the Thomas Alva Edison Foundation in New Jersey. The phonograph was not the only method used to make dolls 'speak': one talking and crying doll of the 1880's was operated by blowing sharply down a tube.

The child of today is offered a variety of speaking dolls: the modern 'Chatty Cathy', for example, says sixteen phrases, ranging from 'I love you, Mummy' to 'When's my birthday?', in a lifelike, if squeaky little voice, by means of a revolving phonograph inside the doll. But it is interesting to note that speaking dolls are still far from cheap; the 'Chatty Cathy' costs nearly six pounds in England, which makes it a luxury toy, rather than the plaything of the average child. Possibly there is no great future in the speaking doll, once the wonder of its attainment has worn off; the average child would probably be quite as content with something that simply squeaks or says 'Mamma' when it leans over. This type of 'squeaking', as opposed to 'speaking', doll has enjoyed prolonged success, being both cheaper to produce, and also gives greater rein to the child's fantasy. Max von Boehm's opinion is that too much mechanical advance in a doll defeats its own purpose, by robbing a child's mind of that essential element of make-believe, which leaves the child free to weave its own dreams around the dummy figure. True or false? I am tempted to agree, having often observed how children will neglect a luxurious doll for something apparently far more ordinary.

108 A group of mechanical dolls made in France about 1860. When wound up, the little girl on the right blows bubbles, the Negro smokes a pipe, the girl on the left lifts the lid of her basket to reveal her shells, and the lady on the far left lifts the lid of her basket which contains a baby lamb.

Walking dolls, like speaking dolls, have a long history, even if once again modern developments have only repeated the ingenious inventions of the nineteenth century. Walking dolls appeared in Paris as early as 1826 [figure 95], and leading doll-makers were eager to take advantage of the novelty; in 1849 a doll appeared with an internal organ which allowed its body to move backward, forward and sideways; and in the 1870's Jumeau produced the 'Jumeau walking doll'. At the Paris Exhibition of 1844, Monsieur Brouillet exhibited dolls which could stand up on their own, if not walk, and at the same Exhibition of 1852, dolls were shown which could actually dance the polka.

109 The clockwork toys made about 1870. When wound up with a key, they roll forward.

In the collection of Mrs Grant J. Holt are two walking dolls from Paris. One is about ten and a half inches tall. She stands on what appears to be a three-wheeled cart without sides, and at the back of this cart is a mechanism which causes the wheels to turn, and the doll appears to be walking. The second doll has an interior mechanism wound with a key, which when released by pressing a lever on the other side of the body, starts two chains going round on opposite sides. These are connected to two rollers under the doll's feet which revolve to make the doll walk. At some point when she is walking, the bellows above the mechanism make a crying sound, and her head moves from side to side as she walks in a lifelike manner. Both these dolls have bisque heads.

It is clear that walking or moving dolls of many different types were the subject of experiment by different manufacturers in France and Germany throughout this period. Although there is a legend that a sailor named Crutchet who fought at Trafalgar was the first to make cheap mechanical toys, simplifying the elaborate clockwork figures which had previously only been within the means of the rich, cheap clockwork toys were always chiefly developed in Europe, and more especially in Germany. Around the cities of Nuremberg and Fürth in particular, this industry flourished, supplying the whole world.

But perhaps the most famous walking doll of the mid-century from the point of view of collectors, was patented in the United States in 1862 [figure 107]. This was the 'Autoperipatetikos' walking doll, which had legs with metal feet that worked by an alternating cant movement when it was wound up. An extract from the directions supplied with the original dolls reads as follows: '1st. With the right hand, wind up, turning the key from you, and then set it LIGHTLY ON ITS FEET...3rd. If it should stop at any time, turn the feet toward you, and see if the inside leg is not caught against the boot. 4th. Do not wind it too tightly.' Obviously the Autoperipatetikos was subject to the usual misadventures of mechanical toys at the hands of uninstructed children and over-eager grown-ups!

Another type of American walking doll put on the market at this time did not need to be wound up at all: she pushed a small cart in front of her and while her head and hands were made of *papier-mâché*, the rest of her was made of metal. She was started on level ground with a little push and moved forward by means of tiny prongs which caught in the hairs of the carpet.

A walking doll of American design and manufacture of much more recent date, was the 'Dolly Walker'. This was invented by Harry Coleman, a ventriloquist on the vaudeville stage, whose dummy travelled around with him. He conceived the idea of

110 A needlework companion doll of 1865 with china head and limbs, 8½ inches high. Here it is shown with a page of Peterson's *Ladies Magazine* of the same date.

copying the mechanism which operated the dummy to the scale of a doll. The original doll had a rather crude body of screen wire and lath, with jointed knees, but later the invention was patented by Mrs Emma C. Clear, of the Humpty Dumpty Hospital, California, and a slender cloth body was made by Mrs Clear's husband at the request of a customer. The Clears had intended to produce the doll on a large scale, when the Second World War put a stop to their plans.

The Wateringbury Watch Company of Connecticut also made a modern American walking doll, which consisted of a boy doll, all metal, about twelve inches tall, with oversized feet concealing a pair of rollers near the heels, similar to those in roller-skates: it walked forward once it had been wound up with the key. But this doll is something of a rarity and probably not a great many were made.

The Schoenhut family, with their wooden dolls, produced a 'Schoenhut Walkable Doll' which had a special arrangement of wires so that by holding it by the arm and proceeding slowly, it actually walked along. Some walking dolls of the present day are propelled by the same method, needing no key to wind them up.

Speaking and walking represent the two main categories by which the manufacturers of the nineteenth and twentieth centuries have attempted to bring further life to their dolls: but beyond these two streams of development lies the whole range of mechanical novelty, continuing in the tradition of the eighteenth century, if not executed with all the craftsmanship of their artists.

A selection of mechanical toys advertised in *New York Fashions* in 1877 gives some idea of the range to be found: 'The mechanical toys imported from Paris are the finest ever brought to this country. The figures are beautiful and correctly costumed, and the motion is perfect. One of these is the Vintager, a peasant, in proper dress, pushing a barrow laden with grapes, while a basket is in his hand and another strapped to his back; when wound up, he moves about the floor for several minutes... The Saucy Milkmaid is propelled rapidly around the room, shaking her head and patting her cow, while the cow munches oats and lows contentedly. The Drunken Muleteer applies the bottle to his mouth with one hand, and holds on to the mule with the other. The Murderous Zouave dashes around the room furiously, snapping a pistol towards the right, then the left, in a most reckless manner...' Yet another old French mechanical toy which reached America, now in a New York private collection, is *Le Gai Violiniste:* the doll is wound up with a key, and then plays the violin in a realistic manner. An eating doll was put on the market in the 1880's which fed on sweets, which then reappeared out of its feet.

Among doll-makers who were interested in mechanical devices, I have already mentioned Bru and Jumeau. Rudolf Steiner, however, a doll-maker from Thuringia, Germany [figure 111], was so keenly interested in this sort of development that he invented as early as 1889 a doll which would drink from a bottle: the bottle had a syphon which then passed right through the length of its head, so that the liquid could be tapped off, as the doll started to 'drink' it, into a receptacle underneath her chair. Yet another flight of fancy in the second half of the nineteenth century was M. Boutard's 'flying' doll.

The moral of the history of automata and mechanical dolls seems to be that once they had passed their imaginative zenith by the end of the eighteenth century, artistry was replaced by an energetic desire for novelty.

111 A German Steiner doll made of china just before the 1914–18 War.

112 *(opposite)* A Breton doll presented to General Eisenhower in 1944 by the people of Brittany.

113 A modern golliwog shown standing by a page from the book that originated the popularity of this soft toy. Although this modern example has a green coat, the original golliwogs all had blue coats like that in the book illustration.

AGAIN AND AGAIN IN CONSIDERING the classic wax, bisque and Parian dolls of the nineteenth century, I have, in common with their collectors, bemoaned the fact that these exquisite materials were so highly fragile. It is scarcely astonishing that the new wave of doll materials after the First World War should have concentrated on durability, or especially, unbreakability.

Among unbreakable materials, rubber enjoyed the first vogue. As early as the 1840's, we find rubber dolls' heads were the subject of experimentation, and many doll patents were con-

114 A modern costume doll from the British West Indies.

cerned with the use of rubber. Thomas Forster improved the use of India rubber by casting it in moulds for the parts of dolls in 1844, and Edward Payne in 1849 moulded and joined hollow figures such as children's dolls. A piece of compound was boiled until it was in a soft state ready for a mould, then the moulds were pressed together by a red hot iron, and the ends trimmed off.

In America Charles Goodyear made experiments with rubber, and in 1851 his brother Nelson Goodyear took out a patent for hard rubber. Goodyear dolls were made in all sizes, and dolls' heads are still found with the legend 'Goodyear Pat. May 5. 1851.' Later, Kammer and Reiner dolls are found with cloth bodies and solid rubber heads and arms, where the colour has been washed into the sap before it is finally modelled.

In the 1920's it gained an additional cachet from the fact that psychologists attached a great importance to the part played in a child's development by correct 'doll-play'. Rubber seemed ideally suited to reproduce a human baby in as lifelike fashion as possible, and it was now felt that these rubber creations represented a far more healthy force in the child's fantasy world than stiff, richly dressed figures of wax or china. Rubber dolls were especially suitable for bathing, feeding and nappy-changing – all the natural functions of the mother towards her baby, which the child might have watched its own mother performing for a younger brother or sister – and also for experiments with the nappy-wetting type of doll, which always fascinates the young!

Akin to rubber for this purpose was celluloid, which was also widely used for baby dolls, on the natural grounds that it was

115 A collection of modern soft toys, hand-made by Margaret Hutchings, a member of the British Toy-makers' Guild.

116 Sacking dolls from Sardinia, made by village women under the direction of Maria Lei, the Italian sculptress.

117 'Friendship' dolls, hand-woven and hand-knitted, given by the Mayor of North Brunswick, Canada, to his friends.

highly washable and therefore sanitary. A compressed solution of nitrated cellulose in camphor, it was originally an English invention, but was actually developed for toy manufacture by an American called Hyatt, and first used for making dolls in the 1880's. The early celluloid dolls were made all in one piece, but jointed dolls with glass eyes, and even sleeping eyes and set-in teeth, followed. Pumice stone was sometimes used in finishing the heads and Carpenter claimed 'a most beautiful and natural look' when the eyebrows were incised and coloured before being rubbed down with pumice stone. A famous American range of celluloid dolls were the Kewpie dolls, with their characteristic happy smiling faces, turned-up noses and kiss-curls on their cheeks, some black Kewpies being also made as Negro babies. However, celluloid toys are apt to crack and dent, disabilities to be weighed up against their washability: a more serious disadvantage still was their inflammability, which no doubt helps to account for their loss of popularity.

Plastic types of doll have largely taken their place as favourites, vinyl being especially successful as a material for dolls, partly because it is washable and therefore hygienic, and partly because it is so cheap to produce in quantity that chain stores in England are now able to sell excellently made vinyl dolls for less than a pound, a price greatly different from the five pounds charged for a Victorian wax doll at a period when money was worth far more. At the same time, more expensive vinyl dolls of higher quality are also produced, two of the best known English firms being Rosebud and Pedigree.

As a contrast to the use of 'washables', comes the revival of the soft toy, such as the hand-knitted doll, or doll made out of fabric or patchwork. Here we may trace a return to the ancient rag doll, whose popularity with the child is certainly perennial. There are two types of modern soft doll; one is the expert soft doll by a hand-made toy-maker, of which there are often exhibitions, and one example of the work of an English crafts-woman is shown illustrated in the present book [figure 115]. Here the workmanship is excellent, and the simplicity of the materials used – knitting wool for hair, boot buttons for eyes, scraps for clothing – is all part of the craft, and intended to appeal to the primitive instinct of the child for something 'easy to love'.

The second type of modern soft toy is far less sophisticated. This is the so-called 'emergent doll', the beloved plaything of the child of the slums, which is made out of very simple materials, because these are the only materials available. Fascinating examples of this type of doll are to be found in the Museum of Childhood, Edinburgh: typical materials used include a wooden spoon, drawn on for the face, a dish mop, dishcloth and napkin ring round the waist to hold it securely together. This type of doll is perhaps nearer in spirit to the very earliest example of doll than to the well-made specimens on show at any display of modern craft handiwork. But what is interesting to observe is that the modern hand-workers are attempting to appeal to the same strong instinct in the child which has produced the 'emergent' doll, or ancient rag doll.

Rag dolls never of course vanished completely from view, even at a time when rag as a material was eclipsed by the splendour of later inventions. There is a theory that Augusta Montanari herself made some rag dolls, as well as her famous waxes, and the nineteenth-century American rag dolls of Izannah F. Walker,

118 *The Doll Shop*, a Victorian painting by A. E. Mulready, showing a little poor girl gazing longingly at the wax and rag dolls beyond her means.

84

120, 121, 122 and 123 *(opposite and right)* A group of four late nineteenth-century French Jumeau dolls at the Brooklyn Children's Museum, New York.

119 A wax portrait-doll of Queen Victoria at her Coronation in 1837.

for which she received a patent in 1873, are now eagerly sought by collectors. Walker dolls' bodies were originally covered in cream sateen, although some examples preserved in collections have been recovered in different materials, due to wear.

A Walker doll, beloved in her childhood, actually inspired another American rag doll-maker, Martha Chase, creator of 'Chase stockinet dolls', and founder of the Chase Doll factory. Chase dolls, although never patented, all bear the label 'The Chase stockinet doll. Made of Stockinet and Cloth. Stuffed with cotton. Made by Hand. Painted by Hand. Made by Especially Trained Workers'. Apart from play-dolls Martha Chase also produced the Chase Hospital Doll, as an aid to teaching nurses, with a watertight interior to enable all the techniques of modern nursing to be practised on it.

Between 1905 and 1910 rag dolls were published in soft cloth books: the pieces were printed on sheets in oils, to be cut out, stuffed and sewn up at leisure at home. Sometimes these dolls were printed on cottons, and sometimes on heavy sateens, and they generally had golden hair, red stockings and black shoes. Some of these dolls, when made up, were actually as high as two and a half feet. Dean's Rag Book Company is well known to connoisseurs as having produced many excellent examples of this kind of doll-cum-book in the early 1900's when they were first made: but the company then found that customers were unwilling to make up the dolls, so the company set about doing it for them, by the same process of stuffing dolls, cut out from cloth sheets. They continued making these dolls until 1958 and are still leading makers of soft toys today; they were from start to finish genuine 'rag' or textile dolls in every particular, with the exception of the hands, which were made of unbreakable material.

124 A Polish doll exhibited at the International Exhibition in Paris in November 1962. It wears a Polish wedding-dress with a flowered crown, real lace pinafore and leather boots.

125 A doll with a china head wearing the bridal costume of the island of Amager, Denmark.

Two interesting fabric doll-makers in Europe were Madame Lenci in Italy, and Frau Käthe Kruse in Germany. The Lenci dolls are highly prized by collectors of the more modern type of doll for their excellence and Madame Lenci made many charming types of dolls, of which the best, in the opinion of experts, were her child dolls. The hallmark of a Lenci doll was the prettiness and good taste of its clothing, Madame Lenci having begun life as an artist. Madame Lenci is dead, but her factory, which closed during the Second World War, has now reopened.

Frau Kruse made a series of baby or toddler dolls in pre-war Germany: her factory also ceased production during the Second World War, when it fell under the displeasure of Hitler, but unlike Madame Lenci, Frau Kruse survived the war, and has now reopened it herself.

Among soft materials both leather and rawhide enjoyed a period of popularity as dolls' materials due to their hard-wearing qualities. We have seen that many very early dolls with wax faces had kid and leather bodies. A number of rawhide dolls were manufactured in America in the 1860's, and in 1866 Franklin J. Darrow of Bristol, Connecticut, was given a patent for the manufacture of dolls' heads from rawhide. The process consisted in cutting the rawhide or untanned leather into round pieces, then steaming it to soften it, then stretching it over moulds. When dry, it was painted. Rawhide was apparently not used for the dolls' bodies, which were made by the home seamstresses who had bought the heads. Rawhide was pretty to look at, and certainly unbreakable: but it turned out to have the unsuspected disadvantage of being highly appealing to rats, which would nibble away at the heads. The heads which have survived to us also have a great deal of the paint flaked away, which suggests another basic weakness.

Indian dolls have of course always been made of leather or kidskin, generally trimmed with beads [figure 14]: there are Indian dolls in private collections of fifty or a hundred years back which look most attractive, trimmed with brightly coloured ornaments, and today it is still possible for the tourist to acquire these modern examples of leatherwork.

A comparatively recent American doll, which achieved fame in the established medium of bisque, was Grace Storey Putnam's Bye-lo Baby doll. Grace Putnam was the widow of a sculptor, who modelled the face of her famous baby doll from an actual three-day-old baby, and achieved an immediate success with it once it came on the market, in spite of initial difficulties in getting manufacturers to accept it. So marked was its popularity – the newspapers calling it 'the Million Dollar baby' – that in New York the company of Borgfeldts who manufactured it, importing the bisque heads from Germany, had difficulty in getting the heads into the country quickly enough.

127 Portrait-dolls of Prince Charles and Princess Anne, children of Queen Elizabeth II, made by Martha Thompson of California. The clothes are hand-made, and the modelling is of exceptional quality.

126 Queen Elizabeth II, a model by Martha Thompson made to commemorate the Coronation. After she had made a certain number of copies, Martha Thompson destroyed the moulds, so that this portrait could not be further duplicated.

But the latter-day history of dolls has not entirely consisted in experimentation with new materials. One of the most significant twentieth-century advances has been the growth in the popularity of the 'mascot doll', which like so many other trends we find prefigured in the production of the early nineteenth-century portrait doll. The portrait doll itself may have stemmed from an earlier fashion prevalent among the rich in the eighteenth century for commissioning lifelike wax portraits of themselves, a fashion to which the success of Madame Tussaud bears witness. Nevertheless, although there are portrait dolls in existence of earlier figures, the first public personality who seems to have been the subject of portrait dolls in large numbers was Queen Victoria [figure 119].

No doubt the happy combination of a young and pretty girl on the throne of a great kingdom, together with the great development at the time in the art of wax doll-making, is responsible for it. Some portrait dolls of Victoria as a young girl already existed before her accession, and wax was not the only material used; in fact, as we have seen, certain china dolls' heads, although not specifically described as portraits, clearly were influenced by her style of looks and hair-style, in the way that modern dolls nowadays tend to resemble the current fashionable film star (the late Marilyn Monroe in particular being responsible for a wave of platinum blonde nylon dolls'

129 Two examples of early child dolls, executed in wax in 1844. The Princess Royal, later Empress of Germany, and Prince Albert Edward, later King Edward VII, the eldest children of Queen Victoria.

128 A Jumeau doll about 1865 with the characteristic large soulful eyes of dolls made by this firm.

130 *(opposite)* The Emperor and Empress of Japan, made about 1880. These are two pieces in a group of dolls known as a *Hina*, or presentation-set, given to brides on their marriage. The *Hina* had some religious significance, and a curtain covered the figures of the Emperor and Empress except on special occasions.

wigs). But the splendid coronation of the Queen produced a variety of reproductions of her image, some being a great deal more lifelike than others, and thereafter the Queen and her numerous young family – Queen Victoria had a total of nine children in fifteen years – provided a constant inspiration to the portrait makers.

Some of the portrait dolls of the young Prince of Wales, Albert Edward, are particularly delightful [figure 68], providing rather a sad contrast with the conventional idea of him as a grown-up, large and portly in his tweed shooting suit, and a fat cigar in the mouth which was once a rosebud. Fortunately his marriage to the beautiful Princess Alexandra of Denmark provided the portrait makers with ample materials from her wedding day onwards. Queen Alexandra, with her wax-like enamelled complexion, and long large eyes set in a neat oval face, already had an appearance of almost doll-like perfection: her hair-styles in particular clearly influenced many nineteenth-century dolls, even if they are not specifically intended to represent her. At the same date in France, the graceful Empress Eugénie both inspired portraits and influenced the design of conventional dolls' heads with her hair-styles, in particular the low braided chignon, which one always associates with her.

Royalty is a natural subject for portrait dolls. As children, the two Princesses Elizabeth and Margaret were subjects for innumerable dolls in the 1930's, some appealing, but some frankly vulgar and clearly intended to attract tourists, lacking all the charm of the wax portraits of the earlier Princes and Princesses. In the same way the Coronation of Queen Elizabeth II appealed to portrait makers [figure 126], much as that of her great-great-

grandmother had done: here one's admiration is aroused by the marvellous workmanship of the Coronation robes, in some cases embroidered with exquisite precision to simulate the original, rather than by any real resemblance to the Queen's face. Perhaps the royal portrait doll was a nineteenth-century art, but merely a twentieth-century curiosity.

America, lacking royalty, did not lack portrait dolls: George and Martha Washington are favourite subjects, although a great many of these, now in collections, are of a far later date than the originals. Martha Chase, already mentioned in connection with her fabric dolls of the 1920's, was particularly fond of representing the Washingtons. The Presidents and their wives were of course natural subjects for portraiture: Thomas Jefferson and Mary Todd Lincoln, wife of Abraham Lincoln, were among popular subjects. It was not surprising to find a wave of 'First Family' dolls in the Kennedy era, with Mrs Jacqueline Kennedy influencing the current American style of doll physiognomy, in exactly the same fashion as Queen Alexandra and the Empress Engénie years previously.

But royal or substitute royal figures are not alone in representation among portrait dolls: other types of public figures also inspired this art. Opera singers, for example, are well represented, and Jenny Lind, the 'Swedish Nightingale', was responsible for numerous wax portrait dolls at the time of her triumphant tour of the United States [figure 71].

Turning from portrait dolls proper to their successors, the mascot dolls, we find that the two earliest examples originated as early as the turn of the twentieth century. The golliwog first broke upon the world in 1895 in Florence Upton's delightful children's best-seller *The Adventures of Two Dutch Dolls and a Golliwog* [figure 113]. Florence Upton apparently was inspired by some grotesque dolls belonging to her grandmother, which had been put away for years: the first book was followed by a number of others in the same series, all celebrating the golliwog, as a result of which it was eagerly reproduced by toy-makers and became a familiar inhabitant of the nursery.

Psychologists sometimes question the wisdom of giving golliwogs to young children on the grounds that the black face, pop-eyes and round red mouth are the unconscious source of many childish nightmares, and set up a series of reactions against black faces which may be of sad social consequence in the world into which the child grows up. On the other hand, surely the fact that most children welcome the golliwog (when awake) with open arms, to say nothing of the immediate popularity of Florence Upton's creation, shows that it corresponds to a definite trend in their affections, which it would be wrong to discourage.

The second early type of mascot doll was of course the teddy bear [figure 138], and here we are on safer ground with the

131 A Danish doll in national dress, wearing the everyday costume of the peoples of Roesnaes, Zeeland.

132 and 133 *(opposite above)* A Danish doll in national dress: a peasant in her Sunday clothes from the island of Fanø. *(below)* A boy doll in Danish national costume.

psychologists, for none has yet questioned the wisdom of giving this eminently soothing object to a young child. It first appeared in 1903, as the result of a cartoon in the *Washington Post* by Clifford Berryman inspired by a newspaper photograph of Teddy Roosevelt in the Rocky Mountains with a little brown bear lying at his feet. At the time there was a border dispute between Mississippi and Louisiana. When the President refused to shoot a bear cub which crossed his line of fire during a bear hunt in Mississippi, this incident appeared as a political cartoon, captioned 'Drawing the Line in Mississippi'. On seeing the cartoon, Morris Michtom, founder of the American firm Ideal Toy Corporation, wrote to the President and asked him if it would be an impertinence for him to make a small bear cub and call it 'Teddy's bear'. According to his son, Mr Ben Michtom, the present President of the Corporation, Roosevelt wrote back to say in effect: 'I don't think my name is worth much to the toy bear cub business, but you are welcome to use it.' Mrs Michtom was deft with the needle and herself helped to make many of the bears, one of which was sent to the President. Others were taken with his letter to Mr Schoonmaker, then buyer for the large wholesaler Butler Brothers, who in 1903 took the entire output and guaranteed Mr Michtom's credit with the mills who supplied the plush. Today there are teddies of every shape, colour and material, and the early emphasis on brown plush has vanished. The present author in her childhood was devoted to a green teddy, grass-green when it arrived, and deepening to a rich bottle-green with age. A traumatic childish memory still lingers round the moment when the beloved teddy was produced at her first school and mocked by the local Establishment for its weird unorthodox colour!

The trail blazed by the golliwog and the teddy bear has been heavily trodden ever since: popular soft toys of a mascot character have since included nearly all the figures from Lewis Carroll's *Alice in Wonderland*, Alice herself being an early favourite for a portrait doll, and Humpty Dumpty outstanding as a soft toy-cum-doll. The tendency is for dolls of this type to spring up in response to the current fashion for a particular children's book, series or character. Thus the *Winnie-the-Pooh* series of A.A. Milne resulted in a wave of Piglets, Christopher Robins and Eeyores. Alison Uttley's *Little Grey Rabbit* series lent itself easily to attractive Squirrels and Hares as well as Little Grey Rabbit herself.

Turning to the world of films, no childhood would be complete without some type of Disney-inspired doll – whether Mickey and Minnie Mouse, so popular before the last war, or Donald Duck or Huckleberry Hound, more fashionable nowadays. Another pre-war Disney favourite was Snow White, who was easy to reproduce in stuffed doll form, with a family of Seven

134 A French Fashion doll made of wax, nearly three feet high, and dated 1899.

135 *(opposite left)* An Armand Marseille doll, dressed in the traditional costume of the London costermonger by Mrs Lily Lodge, the Pearly Queen of Lambeth.

136 *(opposite right)* An American doll of the late nineteenth century, with a china head and the hair of the doll's original owner.

137 Eskimo dolls made of leather and carved wood, and dressed in skins. They were made at Blacklead Island, Baffin Land, under missionary influence about 1910.

Dwarfs round her. Pinocchio, although in origin an Italian puppet, owed his popularity as a toy to a Disney film.

It would be easy to give a long list of such children's favourites, starting back in the 1890's when the Buster Brown series of adventure stories inspired a series of Buster Brown dolls, and continuing to the present day, when at the time of writing, characters in Enid Blyton's stories, pre-eminently Noddy in his pixie cap, are to be found in every English shop, to cater for the demands of children brought up on these books. Since the war, in England, Brumas, the baby polar bear born at the Zoo, and Muffin the mule, the hero of a television series, have been only two examples of toys coming onto the market to follow or exploit the current child's fancy. Another addition to this list of favourite characters has been the Giant Panda of the early 1970's.

The examples vary from year to year and country to country, but the point remains the same: the hold of the doll is so strong on the child's imagination, that if it is captured in some other sphere, he is always delighted to have it transformed into a substantial shape – a shape which he can introduce into his daily life. Perhaps grown-up mascots, such as dolls which dangle in the backs of cars, beflounced telephone dollies and tea-cosy dolls, more common in the 1930's than now, arise from the same urge, transformed for adult forms and tastes.

A more selective adult form of doll-mania is the passion for collecting modern costume dolls from many countries [figure 125], a passion which fits in well with an age when travel, touristic or otherwise, has come within the reach of an increasing number of people. Max von Boehm speaks slightingly of these dolls, saying they bear as much relation to the folklore of the nation which they are intended to represent, as historical novels bear to the history of the time they are intended to portray. The comparison is perhaps a little harsh; or to put it another way, surely both historical novels and contemporary costume dolls have a role to fill which is not to be despised?

Costume dolls from many lands make agreeable subjects to bring home: they are generally well made, present a bright and cheerful appearance, and make more lifelike and more decorative souvenirs than postcards. To compare a modern costume doll to an early wax doll is surely quite unnecessary in estimating its value. Indeed some of the large and detailed collections of costume dolls go further than merely providing colour and stimulating memories: they offer a fascinating guide to the costumes of hundreds of different countries in a most attractive

138 Two teddy bears showing signs of prolonged affection. That on the left is French, and is one of the earliest surviving teddy bears. That on the right is dated 1910.

139 Indian dolls in traditional dress.

form. To collectors a hundred years hence these dolls brought
back in triumph by travellers from such varied places as cheap
African bazaars and glossy European airports, expensive
Parisian shops and South American market places, may represent
treasure trove, as early Dutch dolls and Pennywoods, once so
lightly regarded, do to us now.

The doll collectors of today are indeed sufficiently en-
thusiastic to leave no doubt that this is a passion which will
survive, and continue with undiminished vigour. Doll enthusiasts form in many ways a little world of their own: within
this world, however, they exercise a strong camaraderie, helping
each other to make new discoveries, corresponding with each
other from country to country, and providing a number of
services to fellow enthusiasts in the repair and maintenance of
old dolls which are undreamt of to the outsider. For this world,
doll experts provide the authoritative literature, and even an
abbreviated bibliography of their works would be extensive.

Doll collecting as a passion is at least as old as the seventeenth
century: new to the twentieth century however are the Doll
Clubs, which were initiated in the 1930's, and spread over both
the United States and Great Britain. These clubs not only provide
discussions about dolls and doll collecting among members;
they also perform the valuable service of organizing exhibitions
of dolls for charity, and photographs of various dolls shown at
this type of exhibition are among those reproduced in this
volume.